An Illustrated History of
English Domestic Furniture (1100 -1837)

The Age of the Craftsman

The Age of the Craftsman

Restoration walnut and cane day-bed c.1680.

An Illustrated History of
English Domestic Furniture (1100 -1837)

Ivan Sparkes

SPURBOOKS LIMITED

Published By Spurbooks Ltd
6 Parade Court, Bourne End, Buckinghamshire

© Ivan Sparkes 1980

ISBN 0 904978 34 6

Designed and produced by
Mechanick Exercises, London

Printed in Great Britain by
McCorquodale (Newton) Limited
Newton-le-Willows, Lancashire

Contents

Illustrations

Introduction

The period of English domestic furniture covered in this book shows us an amazing growth in development and design, reflecting the changing shape of society during those centuries. From the Medieval sturdy plank chest to the sophisticated veneered and inlaid Regency commode is a big step, and one which has been recorded many times in other books and periodical articles. In presenting this book, I find myself trying to project a story containing answers to problems I have come across in recognising the basic differences between styles and pieces of English furniture, and in the way in which they have developed.

In so doing, I have found it necessary to read widely and to gather the opinions of authors in different fields of furniture history. Some experts have strong and often differing views from others on the way in which national styles have evolved, and on the part played by the individual craftsmen in the furniture of their period, while others highlight the way in which regional or social factors have governed the introduction of native styles or specific items of furniture.

This book attempts to tread warily between the controversy, but still lists in its bibliography the source books which might help the reader to pursue a particular line of research. To those authors and to the museums I add my thanks.

I.G. Sparkes 1980

1 The Craftsmen — their Tools and Timbers

In 1832 James Hopkinson wrote in his diary, as he prepared to enter the furniture trade as an apprentice, "... my parents should give him £20 and that I should receive no wages the first year, but five shillings per week for the 2nd year, six shillings for the third year, seven shillings for the fourth and eight shillings for the last nine months". In this way James embarked upon a trade or craft in which custom was rife and where the closed shop in many respects existed well over a hundred years ago.

The practice of creating apprenticeships was well established by the time of Elizabeth I, and the conditions were outlined in the Statutes of Artificers of 1563. The Guilds themselves laid down ordinances regarding the dress to be worn and in 1629 the typical apprentice wore a "flat round cap, hair close cut, narrow falling band, coarse side coat, close hose and cloth stockings". The fact that these rules were enforced was apparent in 1619 when an apprentice, appearing before the Wardens of the Turners Company, was ordered to the barber, as he appeared with long hair and curled locks.

Although the Guilds were concerned with the lot of the workman, it was when they felt an injustice was being experienced, or noticed an infringement of their monopoly, that they jumped in with both feet. In the early 13th century demarkation disputes were already common, and it was noted that "While the strength of the joiner's work is dependent upon the firmness and accuracy of making joints, the carpenter relies on the strength, the size and position of the timbers". These timbers could be enormous, and it was quite normal for domestic buildings to use supports fourteen by twelve inches in girth, and in some of the Cathedral buildings, lengths of fifty feet were required. Alan of Walsingham sought far and wide in the country for the right beams for his lantern in the tower of Ely Cathedral.

It is interesting to hear how early the tools which were still in use in the 18th and 19th century were brought into practice. When Thomas Vyell died, his will of 1472 included his working tools. "Also I bequeath to Thomas my son myn splyting saw (rip saw), brood axe (broad axe), a luggyng belt (adze), a ffellyng belte (felling axe), a twybyll (pole axe or mattock), a squier (square for lining up edges), mortys wymbyll (auger or brace for boring holes), a foote wymbyll (large auger) a drawte wymbyll (auger with a guide), a compas (compass or divider), a handsawe and a kytting saw (cross-cut saw)." Historical references to tools record that the axe was in use in 1406, called a 'merkyngaxe' for marking timber, and in

1477 the 'axe called a froward' which was most likely the *froe* which is used in the rural woodcrafts for splitting timber lengthways. The adze was used at Hestormel Castle in 1343 for "smoothing old timber because the timber was so full of nails".

The list of tools at the Westminster Lodge in 1444 included the 'puttesawe' or pit-saw and a saw called Kytter which was most probably a framed pit-saw. In 1423 the 'tenonsawe' appears, while when Hengrave Hall was being built in 1535 'sawyepitts' were made at Sowe Wood nearby. Other tools include the 'handhamer and clouehamer' in 1473, and there was a "great lathe for carpenters" at Dover in 1320. For finishing the wood surfaces the rough skin of the dog-fish was used in place of sandpaper in 1355, and the glue-pot was filled with fish-sound in 1348.

The disputes between the various craft guilds continued and in 1632 the Joyners stipulated that "all work that had mortesses or tennants or that was duftalled, pynned or glued, and all sorts of wainscott and sealing of homes (i.e. panelling) also all carved workes either raised or cutt through or sunk in with the grounde taken out being wrought and cutt with carving tools without the use of plaines . . . came into their hands". In a similar way the Worshipful Company of Turners possessed the exclusive right of "making thrown chairs, stools, wooden bowls, trays, measures, spinning wheels and all kinds of ship's fittings, such as deadeyes, blocks and sheaves".

An example of how this could be by-passed by the joiners is seen in those gateleg tables of the 17th century where the turned baluster leg supporting the main central trestle is replaced with a splat cut to the same outline but in the flat. However, don't assume that the Joiners and the Turners had everything their own way, for they must have been in sympathy with the Upholsterers in 1689 when the latter drew up a petition against the newly introduced cane chair. We find the Upholsterers of Bedford complaining that "since cane chairs have been in use, the trade hath decayed, and is lost, now the said Poor, that used to be employed, beg their bread; and the town and others near without some redress will come to Ruin".

Another cause of hardship for the craftsmen lay in the number of foreign craftsmen who came across the Channel for work, or were fleeing from religious persecution in their own countries. Certainly the names of craftsmen employed in some of the undertakings in this country, particularly where fine carving was required, indicate foreign origins. In 1517 one "poore carpenter" pleaded that "In this season, the Genoese, Frenchmen and other strangers, said and boasted themselves to be in such favour with the King . . . and the multitude of strangers so great in London that the poor English artificers could scarce get any living".

Expertise of the craftsman was of prime importance to the Guilds and Companies, and each artisan in the Turner's Company, before he could set up as a masterman, would serve seven years as an apprentice, followed by two more as

Workshop in the 18th century, showing frame-saw in use and carver at work. From
'Dictionnaire des arts et metiers' 1763.

a journeyman, and then had to produce proof pieces before he could join the
Company. In fact the Company installed a lathe and cuttings tools in its
premises to ensure that the proof-piece was completed un-aided.

Not all boys started off as apprentices. When William Parnell was questioned
in 1888 during the *Sweating Shop's Commission* he said, "There is scarcely a
legally bound apprentice in London now at present. Boys go into the shops as
errand boys, to sweep up the shavings and run errands for the men, and in a little
while as they get bigger and stronger, they get a jack-plane put in their hands,
and as they assist the men . . . they pick up a knowledge of the trade". Such boys
also started at an early age, often doing work after school in order to earn money.
A child could earn a penny per week for chairpacking. One lad started working
from 4.30 pm to 7.30 pm making wooden wedges; these were split with the grain
and dried on the stove, and he was able to make a gross an hour for a penny a
gross (144 items). In a town like High Wycombe in Buckinghamshire, most of
the boys ended up in the trade, and of the fifty two children who left the British
School in 1854, twenty two went into chair factories. For those who *were*
indentured, the parchment document was both a straight-jacket and a way to
success. The provisions remind us that the proposed apprentice "shall not
commit fornication nor contract matrimony within the said term, he shall not
play cards or dice tables or any other unlawful games wherebye his masters may

13

have loss with his good or otherwise, he shall neither buy nor sell, he shall not haunt taverns nor playhouses".

In return for his abdication of most of a young lad's pleasures, the master promises "to find, provide and allow the said apprentice, competent and sufficient meat, drink, apparel, lodging, washing and other things necessary and fit for an apprentice" and of course it was the master or his wife who decided what was actually "fit". James Hopkinson recalls one boy who was an indoor apprentice and the Mistress used to make many meat and potato pies in a dish. He got quite tired of them in time, and also thought there was not enough meat in them anyhow. So he got a long clean board, and put along the length of it pieces from his pies, counting out ten pieces of potato to one piece of meat all the way up the board. The master came in and asked him what he was doing. He replied, "I'm counting out my one in ten pie Sir!" and he didn't get many such pies after that.

When Thomas Parker of Parker Knoll started work in London in 1894 he earned one shilling a week, of which his dinner at the corner cookshop of beef and potatoes cost him seven pence a week with an extra halfpenny for bread.

Besides the normal mealtimes, illegal dinners were often planned. "One time the master came in just as we were frying kidneys and mutton chops about 11 o'clock in the morning. The door was fastened on the inside, and no one could get in until it was opened to them. We had a private knock so when we heard this strange knock we were in such a fix to know what to do with the frying pan. At last one of the men opened his workchest and popped it in, frizzling away being just taken off the fire . . . so that when the master was let in we were all busily at work. He kept smelling about, but did not say anything, and at last he went away".

The craftsman's working hours have always been long; in medieval times the winter hours were 5.00am to 7.00pm, and in the summer they extended to 8.00pm. However there was a most generous time allowance for a midday meal known as *noschenes* and for a more familiar custom called *drinkynges*. In the summer months a period was put aside in the afternoon for the *sleepynges* and this, with lunch, sometimes extended to three and a half hours. By the 1870s the hours had changed very little, and it was really the men's approach to work which dictated whether they seemed long or short. The actual hours were about sixty per week, one chairmaker recalls that they were "at our benches six o'clock and did not leave off work until eight o'clock pm, including Saturday" but this was a rather dismal and sad remembrance. Another workman from the same town recalls that "work started anything from 5.30 to 6.00am, breakfast being taken at 7.30 to 8.00am, then at 10.00am those who were not teetotallers, and they were few, took ten minutes for beer and bread and cheese, often accompanied by a good strong onion. From 12.00 to 1.00 we had dinner, and 3.30 to 4.00pm tea. After that work would go on until 7.00pm.

14

This tradition of long hours persisted into the present century. As recently as 1934 a furniture firm was taken to court for working a young lad on Thursday from 7.30am to 6.30pm, then back the same evening from 10.30pm to 4.00am, and back once more at 10.00am until 4.00pm the next day.

Whether the youngsters came in as apprentices or as boy workers, they still had to be taught the work. James Hopkinson recalls that "having cut out the wood for the table, I was told that I must pay a shilling for them to drink my health, and also that they expected my father to pay a sovereign towards a binding supper... and for every fresh job that I had not made one like it before, I had to pay a shilling or I should not have been allowed to make it. For every shilling got in this way, every man in the workshop had to put down 1½d whether *he* liked it or not, and as I was the youngest apprentice, I had to fetch the drink from the public house".

The relationship between the workers and the masters varied from workshop to workshop, but I feel the Utopian situation in the 18th century premises of Mr. Sedon was unusual. Sophie von la Roche, writing in 1786 states, "We drove first to Mr. Seddon's, a cabinet-maker, and before leaving for Windsor I must tell you a little about our unusual visit there. He employs four hundred apprentices on any work connected with the making of household furniture — joiners, carvers, mirror-workers, upholsterers, girdlers — who mould the bronze into graceful patterns, and locksmiths. All these are housed in a building with six wings. Seddon, foster father to four hundred employees, seemed to me a respectable man, a man of genius, too, with an understanding for the needs of the needy and the luxurious; knowing how to satisfy them from the products of nature and the artistry of manufacture; a man who has become intimate with the quality of woods from all parts of the earth, with the chemical knowledge of how to colour them or combine their own tints with taste, and has appreciated the value of all his own people's labour and toil, and is for ever creating new forms".

This is a different picture from that presented in the provincial town. "A particular annoyance was *light money*. The windows of many of the workshops were not glazed but covered with calico or light hessian which made artificial light necessary quite early in the winter evenings. The charge for oil for the lamps was sometimes 8d. a week for each man, and when one boss introduced gas lighting, he still made a charge of 6d. a week. A further charge was for *benchroom*, and this could be 2/- a week... in a similar way the workmen would demand a new man pay his *footing* a sum of 2/-, before they would allow him to commence any job". The workman had to supply his own tools, and also had to pay the employer 2d. a week for the use of the grindstone to sharpen them, and further ½d. a week was contributed towards the services of the errand boy who fetched and carried for them.

The employer's view of the workmen was also not always complimentary. "In many cases they were unable to alter their method of work, and in others they

Cutting veneers in the 18th century workshop. From *'Dictionnaire des arts et metiers* 1763.

flatly refused to have anything to do with work they were not used to". Writing in 1880, Manfred Bale said, "The great cost and in some cases, the inferior quality of work turned out by hand, have rendered the increasing introduction of labour-saving machinery absolutely necessary to keep pace with the general prosperity of the times".

There were always some workmen who were good craftsmen, but even they were sometimes bribed to move from workshop to workshop. "If a man was offered a farthing an hour rise, he would dance, if he had a halfpenny an hour rise, he would jump with joy."

The type of work and the ease with which it was undertaken was of course largely dependent upon the timber used, and over the years fashion and scarcity made great changes in the materials used in furniture making. Oak was at first the most popular, with William Harrison writing in the 17th century, "Nothing but oak was any whit regarded", and Evelyn in his book on timbers entitled *Sylva*, "It is doubtless of all timber hithertoe known the most universally useful and strong". The wood is hard and heavy, and in this country the common oak, *Quercus robur*, or the fruited oak, *Quercus sessiliflora*, were mostly used. The timber used in most surviving medieval English furniture is oak, and the extensive forests of this country were thickly stocked with it. Mature timber was cut in great quantities and not only did the replacement of young trees not keep up with demand, but the period of growth, being up to 250 years, meant that as

16

early as 1233 there were complaints of the difficulty of finding really good timber in the Forests of Windsor and Cornbury. The rapid reduction of the forest areas caused an Act to be passed under Henry VIII to ensure the preservation of oak woods. This shortage of oak was to some extent countered by the import of oak from abroad. The Customs records of ports on the East coast show imports of timber from the Baltic ports, and in 1360, 60 boards called *way-shot*, a term more usually known as *waynescottes,* were brought for 10 shillings at Barton-on-Humber. In 1500 the ship *Cristofer* brought from Danzig to Newcastle 2,400 *clapholt* and the *George* brought 1,500 *waynsketts* and 4,400 *clapholt* which indicates a good traffic in imported timber. This imported oak was also approved of by Evelyn, who agrees the English oak was the choicest timber for decorative work "till the finer grain'd Spanish and Norway Timber came amongst us, which is likewise of a whiter colour".

Oak is generally difficult to work, owing to its coarse and uneven texture, and was probably used before the other timbers because it was easy to split with a wedge at a time when the tree trunks were riven rather than sawn. So, although medieval furniture was made chiefly of oak, by the end of the 17th century it became restricted to the construction of the underlying carcase and the drawer linings. As a rider, Evelyn's comment about the imperfections of oak are interesting, he notices that "oak will not easily glew to other wood, nor not very well to its own kind".

In the past, the history of furniture has been comfortably divided according to the material used, thus we have the *Oak Period* which takes us from medieval times up to the Restoration, when the *Walnut Period* commences.

Convenient as this might appear to the art historian, many other woods were in use at the same time. In the 13th century a number of fir or deal boards were imported and used for building.

Reference was made to a great counter 13ft. long by 12ft. broad designed for the Exchequer at York in 1320 when 18 boards of fir (or deal) were used to board it. Beech occurs, and elm, a timber which is often disparaged due to its tendency to warp, was in constant demand in the Middle Ages. Other timbers in use include poplar, used in a wardrobe at Dunster in 1405, willow, used for a manger at Cambridge Castle in 1295, and ash and lime also appear, but used more for tool handles and in building.

Walnut, however, has been a wood for furniture for many years, and although it did not begin to replace oak until after the Restoration, the King's Hall account for 1491 has a sum of 3s. 6d. for *sawying unius walnotetre et hewyng* (for sawing one walnut tree and hewing) and in 1536 twenty-four loads of walnut and ash timber were sent to Windsor Castle, presumably for furniture making. The prized veneers had the burr markings which occur often at the base of the tree where the fibres are contorted and numbers of small knots give an attractive pattern when the veneers are matched.

Two types of walnut were used in England, *Juglans regia* and *Juglans nigra*, and walnut timber was imported from France in the early 17th century, but after the Restoration the imports grew, until the severe winter of 1709 destroyed many of the walnut trees in central Europe. Then came the more regular imports of the black walnut from Virginia in the mid to late 18th century, until we find in 1786, *Chambers Encyclopædia* reporting that it was held in great esteem "till the quantity of mahogany and other useful woods, which have in late years been imported into England, have almost banished the use of it".

The use of mahogany was known in England as early as 1671 but it was not until the 1730s that it was imported in large quantities, following the change in import duties in 1721. It is a hard and heavy wood; its great width made it ideal for table tops and its strength allowed the use of open *fret* or *cutwork*, essential in making very slender items of furniture. The extent to which it was used in the 18th century was commented upon by Rochefoucauld on his visit to England in 1784. "It is remarkable that the English are so much given to the use of mahogany; not only are their tables generally made of it, but also their doors and seats and the handrails of their staircases." He added that the tables to which he referred were "made of most beautiful wood and always have a brilliant polish like that of the finest glass".

Even mahogany had its limitations, and was displaced by satinwood and other light-coloured woods in about 1770. These finer woods were for the richer householder, for most of the population were quite happy to have their furniture made of ash, beech, chestnut, elm, yew and cedar, and the many fruit-trees which were close at hand, but it is probably due to this fact and their tendency to attract worm and thereby decay, that so few pieces of furniture in these woods have survived in any quantity to this day from the medieval period.

The timber has been cut in the forests of England, but in many cases it has not been replaced to any great extent. As late as the end of the 19th century the chair manufacturers of High Wycombe had little interest in re-afforestation, leaving such things to nature. One who thought differently acquired four hundred acres of woodland, cut down two hundred trees a year and always planted at least two thousand. But the returns on such planning are slow ". . . my father lived to 84 and I suppose in his lifetime must have planted at least forty thousand trees, and he cut down five, and they were only small trees".

In this use of various woods, it is interesting to hear of Roger de Multon who, in 1317, brought an action to court against two carpenters he employed to build a house made of oak. Unfortunately he detected that some of the out-of-sight timbers were made of alder and willow. The carpenters were fined six pence, and Roger received damages to the value of two shillings. Surely an early example of the use of the modern Trades Description Act.

② Tables

The introduction of furniture into the domestic scene was a long process, as it was only when a need arose, and the craftsmen were prepared to interpret that need, that any useful and attractive pieces of furniture materialised, and a more comfortable house interior evolved. The starting point takes us back to the medieval period in England, when the hall formed the main part of the manor house, and when a very communal master-servant relationship existed which allowed the various stratas of society to live together without friction. There was little room for niceties in the form of table manners or cleanliness, and certainly no place for prudery when the undressing and bedding arrangements, as with most other functions, formed part of the open living arrangements of the hall.

Most households, whether that of provincial merchant or of nobility, were very similar in arrangement. Given any room with its size, it is possible to look at the detailed inventories which have survived from the 16th century, and say with fair accuracy, how it was furnished.

The hall was usually a bare large room, probably with a central open fire, the smoke billowing into the roof among the rafters. A main table, generally on a dais would stand at the end of the hall, with a side table extending from it at right angles into the body of the room. When William Cely was in Calais, lodging with other merchants at an Englishman's house, there was an argument over their payment for food, and he writes, "We schulde payne noo more for owre burdd but IIIs IVd a weke at the hye tabull and IIs VIIId at the syde tabull".

It seems that the table is one of the earliest items of furniture to emerge from this period, but it is unlikely that any of great antiquity have survived in England. If they were common in the 13th century, it is surprising that none seems to have survived in the way other 13th century woodwork has, for as early as the end of the 12th century a chair is noted as part of the furniture of a well appointed bedroom. So it is possible that Donald Smith's view is correct, which traces the table back to *butts* or sawn portions of trunks of trees standing on end on the hall floor, on which plank tops, tongued and grooved or fixed together with dowels and cross pieces were laid.

This principle, somewhat similar to that of the butcher's block, may have preceded the trestle table which was one of the first in a series of early table types. The top of the table took its name from the Anglo-Saxon word *bord*, i.e., a board which was brought out for meals, placed on trestles and then put away

after the meal was over. From this original use come the phrases *the festive board,
bed and board* and the still more common term of *boarding house.*

Elm was frequently used for these great table tops, up to three feet in width
and six inches thick, for although elm is not as durable as oak, it grows more
quickly. When oak was used, little of it was converted into planks by saw prior to
the latter part of the 16th century, instead the medieval method was to use the
beetle and wedge and then the split oak was trimmed with an adze. The tree is
first quartered in the direction of its length, and the quarter is cut into planks in
cuts which follow the radiating lines known as the medullary rays. The ensuing
boards are not as wide, but were considered to have superior hardness, durability
and freedom from warping.

TRESTLE TABLES: 14th—18th Centuries

As the whole household dined together, temporary trestle tables would be placed
in position down the hall with forms and stools arranged around them. The early
trestle tables (and note that the term *table* refers to the table-top) were supported
on heavy *trestles* or *horses* constructed from solid wood which were made in three
types. One was in the form of a central pillar rising from heavily constructed
cross-feet, which acted in the same way as the centre support of a Victorian
round table. A second type was constructed from solid square timbers in an
'I'-shape, with an upper and lower heavy bar or rail joined vertically by a massive
square pillar upright, often ornamented with carved or shaped supports. The
third type does not appear to have survived the Medieval period, but is
illustrated in manuscripts as a triangular shape.

These trestle tables appear to date from the 14th century, but very early, round
trestle tables existed in the 10th century, as they are depicted in the Bayeaux
Tapestry (1066-77) where William the Conqueror is shown dining with Bishop
Oda. In their later form, they would not have been easily transportable as it
would have taken several men to move them. Originally it was necessary for most
furniture to be moveable, as an army, marching through the country, would
spare little that came its way. Even in peaceful times, the outbreak of fire must
have been an ever present danger, and with the fire burning in an open hearth in
houses made of timber, little would survive the holocaust. Other reasons for
needing to move furniture quickly would be when the household moved from
one property to another, or to allow valuable furniture to be stored when not in
use or, when, for instance, the hall was cleared for some important event.
Froussart states that the tables were *raised* (i.e. removed) if the King of England
or ladies remained in the hall, as their lingering after a meal indicated the need
for space for dancing and other entertainments. The trestle table was used well
into the 18th century, and among Charles I's furniture at Greenwich was "a long
table standing upon antique tressells". At times the trestle table was not as steady

as it should have been, and in a letter written by Sir Dudley Carlton in 1605, he mentions that at a banquet he attended, the guests were so boisterous that the food "was so furiously assaulted that down went tables and trestles before one bit was touched". The trestle tables became graceful by the 16th century, designed with pierced trestles and the board having its edges richly carved. The tables were used by diners sitting on one side only, the other side was used for serving — but this meant having to use extremely long tables when a large number of guests was present. In time these loose tables were replaced by more permanent ones, later known as *joyned*, but at the time referred to as the *table dormant*. In an oft quoted reference, Geoffrey Chaucer (1340-1400), comments on the hospitality of the Franklen:-

His table dormant in his halle alway,
Stood redy covered at the longest day.

DORMANT TABLES: 15th—17th Centuries

With the dormant table, the two or more trestles were linked together with a heavy cross timber, in the form of a stretcher which gave it rigidity and which also allowed the size and weight of the original trestles to be reduced. Each end of the stretcher was *tusk-tenoned* through the trestle-upright with the tenon protruding the other side to be pegged and secured. This term *dormant* appears in inventories and the phrase "one long table and dormans in the Hall Chamber" appears as late as 1686 in an inventory of Edward Allen. A good example of the dormant table with oak frame and trestles with an elm top c.1600 is in the Ipswich Museum.

The size of these tables would vary from the normal length of six feet to some banquet tables, such as the two trestle tables at Penhurst Place in Kent, said to date from the 14th century, which measure twenty-seven feet in length and about three feet wide. The rough finish of table tops was often concealed beneath a diapered table cloth, and inventories indicate that a table cloth might measure six yards in length. These cloths almost touched the floor on all sides, and would be carefully ironed into sharp creases, or, on festive occasions, draped in swags.

The meals at feast times could be enormous. In 1258 the Queen celebrated the feast of St. Edward, and the town of High Wycombe was ordered to supply bread to the value of £10 for Whitehall, when four loaves cost one penny. The feast arranged in 1466 when George Nevill was made Archbishop of York makes all others shrink into insignificance. It included "300 tuns of ales, 100 tuns of wine, 104 oxen, 6 wild bulls, 1,000 sheep, 304 calves, 2,000 pigs, 304 swine, 400 swans, 2,000 geese, 1,000 capons, 400 plovers, 100 dozen of quails, 200 dozen of the bird called 'rees', 104 peacocks, 4,000 mallard and teal, 204 cranes, 204 kids, 2,000 chicken, 4,000 pigeons, 4,000 crays, 304 bitterns, 400 herons, 200 pheasants, 500 partridge, 400 woodcocks, 100 curlew, 1,000 egrettes, 500 stags, bucks and roes, 4,000 cold venison pasties, 1,000 'parted' dishes of jelly, 3,000 plain dishes of jelly, 4,000 cold baked tarts, 1,500 hot venison pasties, 2,000 hot custards, 608 pikes and bream, 12 porpoises and seals.''

Quite often only certain parts of the meal were served on plates, instead loaves of bread, cut into thick slices called *trenchers* were handed round, and portions of meat with gravy were served straight on to the bread. The guests would cut up the meat and the gravy would soak into the trencher, and these, after the meal, would be given to the poor.

Table manners were not widely practised in these times, for a French metrical poem of the 15th century *'Contenances de Table'* advises the gentlemen not to spit on the table, rather on to the floor, similarly, when he is washing out his mouth with water or wine, it was more proper to spit it on to the floor rather than back into the basin. We find also that the wine not used was thrown on the floor, and in fact the benches and seat were often so dirty that the poet also advised the student to look carefully at his seat before sitting down to a meal!

JOYNED TABLES: 16th—17th Centuries

The trestle tables gave way to the *dormant table,* and this in its turn, by the early 16th century, was replaced by the *joyned* or *framed* table, sometimes called the *long table.* The familiar heavy table top is now supported by four, six or more heavy turned legs which are linked either by a square sectioned continuous stretcher about two inches off the floor, jointed into the legs and pinned with dowels, or the 'H' shape stretcher with two end rails and a central rail running along the centre of the length of the table. A frieze, several inches deep is jointed in the same way around the top of the legs, thus forming a substantial underframe which is fixed to the table top by oak dowel pins driven into the framework. An inventory of Sir William More of Losely for 1556 refers to such a table as "a table of chesnut with a frame joynd to the same".

The earlier types of tables have been chiefly the work of the carpenter, but now we find the new joyned tables involving in their construction, the joiner, the woodturner and the carver. The very nature of the joyned table, with its more even distribution of legs and with the strengthening timbers of the frieze and stretchers, gave us a more substantial table, which, due to its size, was also called the *long table.* When set in the hall or parlour, they were, in the words of the diarist John Evelyn (1620—1706) "as fixed as the freehold".

The timber used in the construction included beech, oak or elm, and records for 1249 show how Henry III ordered a great beech tree to be sent to London to be converted into tables for the kitchens at Westminster for the Eastertide banquets. From this we can assume these would have been trestle tables brought in to provide surfaces for the preparation of the great feasts. Still earlier, during

22

Joyned table with chamfered square legs and floor level continuous stretcher, early 17th century.

the reign of Richard I (1189—1198), payments were made to carpenters at the King's Hall at Portsmouth, for sawing trunks of trees and shaping the planks into tables. With so many demands on English timber, we find that as early as the 14th century, oak was being imported from the Baltic, notably from Danzig. From Norway came *firre-deales*, and walnut from France and Spain. In 1253 we find that the Sheriff of London contracted to "buy 3,000 Norway boards and half a hundred of great boards in their bailiwick to make tables, and carry them without delay to Windsores for delivery to the keepers of the King's Works there to use as the King has enjoined".

In its original form, the timbers of the table were not necessarily stained, being a rich brown colour, but during the Victorian period, G. Bernard Hughes believes they were stained black, and many reproductions were also made at the same period. It should be noted, however, that most Jacobean furniture has come down to us coated in this black patena, so perhaps the smoke, grime and furniture wax of the ages have achieved this finish.

The legs were joined at the top to the deep frieze which was decorated with carving ranging from simple reedings and vertical flutes to rosettes within squares and lunettes. When the table was constructed to be used against a wall, more as a serving table, it was quite normal for only the front and sides to be carved, with the back plain. The shallow lunette carving and vertical gouging were typical of the 16th and early 17th centuries.

The ornamentation of the legs of the joyned table is a good guide to dating, for the changing fashions of the heavy bulbous carved legs are most distinctive. The round bulb shape is believed to be of Flemish or Dutch origin, introduced into

23

England by immigrant craftsmen, but also through the published designs of De Vries and Dietterlein.

At first the legs were quite plain, cut square and sometimes chamfered on the inner corners. Other plain designs included a faceted vase form of hour-glass or hexagonal shaping. The bulb however, which became most popular, was built up by gluing rectangles of wood around a square central post, the basic shape could then be turned on a pole lathe, and the intricate details carved at the bench. The shape which emerged was known as the *cup and cover,* with very thinly turned upper and lower connected necks. They were deeply carved, either with acanthus leaves or gadroons. The bulb was heaviest about 1580 and was reduced in size and the deepness of the carving by about 1630. The plain turned legs were in vogue again in the mid 17th century, and at that time the fluted leg was also popular, with the vase shaped turning more noticeable in the late 17th century.

There are several opinions as to the probable datings of these designs, which effected table legs, chair legs, and baluster turnings on cupboard furniture, but in general the turnings can be linked in the following way:

Bulbous leg 1575-1650
Column form (plain turned or hexagonal) 1590-1690.
Vase-turned 1640-1710
Twist or spiral turning (Barley sugar) 1660-1700
Bobbin turning 1640-1700
Inverted cup 1689-1705

THE DINING TABLE: 16th Century onwards

It appears that the idea of living communally in the hall began to pall in the late 15th century, and we find the practice arising whereby the Lord and his family began to dine away from the household, in a separate room. This habit was from the first frowned upon, and in 1526 Bishop Grosbeske denounced "eating in corners and secret places". As the country became more prosperous in the 16th century, we find farmers, yeoman and the rising generation of merchant families building their houses with both hall and parlour. Dr. Andrew Boorde, writing in 1547 advised his readers to "make the hall of such fashion that the parlour be annexed to the head of the hall, and the buttrye and pantrye at the lower end thereof". The extent of this new fashion appears in an estimate from figures in *'Farm Cottage Inventories of Mid Essex 1635-1749'* where out of 245 houses listed, 209 still had halls but over 183 had invested in a parlour.

Using the smaller room required somewhat smaller furniture, and it was necessary to use a table which would look attractive in such circumstances. The contemporary joyned and trestle tables were somewhat overpowering, and it was soon found that a cut-down verison, while adequate for the family, was of little

24

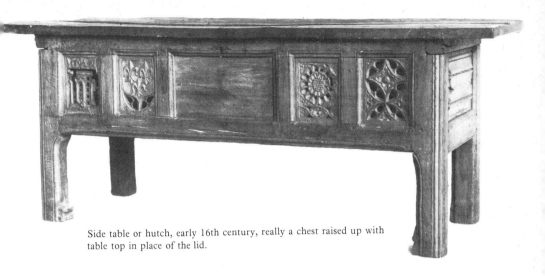

Side table or hutch, early 16th century, really a chest raised up with table top in place of the lid.

use when guests arrived. This problem, according to R.W. Symonds, was soon solved, as he dogmatically states that "by the reign of Elizabeth all forms of table extensions had been invented, and nothing new has since been thought of".

THE DRAW-TOP TABLE: 1550—1650

The method of overcoming the problems of the long table, was by the use of a hinged-leaf, a draw-leaf, or a separate leaf. There is some doubt as to the earliest of the first two types, as we find R.W. Symonds illustrates a *hutch table* which he dates as belonging to the first half of the 16th century, having a place for two folding top flaps which could be supported by wooden supports known as *lopers*, drawn out of the ends of the table. This particular type of furniture was a small serving table with a cupboard below the table top which seems to have evolved from the *hutch* or *chest*. An early reference to such a table is in an inventory of 1534 "a new foldon table of waynescotte wt cofers lockyd in it". A much earlier reference which goes back to the 14th century is quoted by R.W. Symonds, where tables are referred to as 'foldyn' but it is possible that the trestle rather than the table-top performed this action.

In general the first of the extending tables was known as the *draw table*, the *drawing table* or the *draw-top table*. Here the extended top separated into three leaves, of which the outer two leaves slid down underneath the centre leaf when not in use. The advantage of this type was in the fact that either or both of the two end leaves could be used at any time, and when not in use, the spare leaves were concealed and out of the way. The runner or *raking bearers* which supported the draw leaves when extended were called *swords* and it is possible that they evolved from the *lopers* which were used earlier on the folding tables. These runners were tapered so that when the draw leaves were pulled out, they enabled the leaves to rise to the same level as the table top and so create a level flush surface.

This draw-table was a most ingenious invention, probably coming from the Continent, and one which appeared in England in the middle of the 16th century. One early reference of 1553 mentions "a fayer drawing table of wallnuttree vpoon iiij carved pillors of the same stuffe". The varieties of carving and of leg design which were to be found in the construction of the joyned table were now applied to the draw-table. They were considered pieces of importance; many were richly decorated with high quality carving and were often made of walnut and other fine woods. The height of the draw-table was usually 2ft 9ins, its length would be 6ft when closed and up to 11ft when opened. During the Commonwealth Period, a number of the elaborate altars in churches were removed, and plainer tables put in their places. In this way draw-tables and shorter joyned tables have survived in circumstances where they might otherwise have been replaced or cannibalised into making later furniture. The draw-tables, the joyned table and the trestle table all continued to be made, and it was the introduction of the *fall-top* or *gate-leg* table, which caused them to go out of use early in the 17th century, not to be revived with any popularity until the 20th century.

FOLDING TABLES: 1500—1650

The tables which followed and also superseded the draw-tables were known as gateleg tables after the nature of the supporting leg which swung out from the main chassis of the table to support the spare table leaf. They were of two kinds, those with a hinged flap which folded back on top of the fixed table leaf, and those with a hanging flap which was lifted up to the level of the table top and supported by the gateleg. The former were often termed *folding tables* and the latter *falling tables*.

The early folding tables had semi-circular half-tops supported on three legs, and the flap, which was also semi-circular, folded away over on to the solid top. The gateleg was made by vertically halving one of the rear legs and hinging it on the upper frieze and fixing it also with a hinge to the lower straight rear stretcher, which with the front semi-circular stretcher made the table rigid. Sometimes there was a *well* below the rigid half within the depth of the ornamental frieze, in which the table-cloth, gamesboards and dice could be kept. These tables also existed in octagonal shape, and as a number have been found in use in churches, they have frequently been called *credence tables*. They were known in the 15th century in their earliest form, and in 1502 John Coote of Bury

St Edmunds bequeathed his "best faldyn table" from his hall to a relative, and in the *Rutland Accounts* of 1589, a payment of 36s. was made for a "foldinge round table" which measured 10½ft. in circumference. The turnings on the early tables which have survived are plain columns with rings top and bottom, and the semi-circular frieze is carved in light relief in geometrical patterns, c.1620. Only slightly later, such tables have the *halved* leg in the gateleg section replaced with a full baluster leg and the frieze has been arcaded under the framing, and the plain column of the legs changed to the vase-shaped or the bobbin turned baluster. In all examples of the folding table, the main part of the table is a solid structure to which the hinged top and the gateleg are attached, and this type of table continued to be made up to about 1650, when the gateleg table with the falling leaf seems to have taken over.

Early 17th century folding side table, the gate-leg supports the semi-circular fold-back top.

FALLING TABLE OR GATELEG TABLE: 1600 onwards

Although an early reference to the gateleg has been found in an inventory of 1600 "a little table of wainescott with two fallinge leaves" it seems probable that it emerged for general use in the mid 17th century. The early tables which have survived repeat the basic pattern of a central narrow fixed leaf with two wide flaps which fall almost to the floor and which were supported by two hinged gatelegs. The tables made from 1600 to 1660, whether large or small seem to have the central fixed leaf supported at each end by a single upright which might be shaped out of flat timber, cut rectangular or turned, and which was made steady by trestle feet held firm by a broad stretcher rail which linked two trestles, just clearing the floor.

These gateleg tables were usually oval, as the depth of the falling leaf tended to create this shape, and with early examples the width of the centre fixed leaf was 2ft 6ins and the height 5ins to 6ins lower than the early long tables of the period. It is possible that they were used beside a chair or bed as a surface to hold a candlestick or drinks. The *gates* were often quite plain, both uprights and

Oak gate-leg table c.1670 with ball and ring baluster turned legs, two falling leaves to convert it into a round table.

stretcher, and it was not until the Restoration that the elaborate turnings with which we are familiar in modern Victorian reproductions, came into vogue. The top and bottom of the gate in some post-Restoration tables swing on an elaborate wooden hinge, while in most the pivot is more common. The join between the rigid centre leaf and the falling leaves was originally square-cut, but in the late 17th century the *rule joint* was introduced. This gave a convex and concave moulding at the edges which closed and opened over each other, and so concealed the hinge itself. These hinges were of wrought iron, either square or butterfly shaped, and fitted into position with hand-wrought nails. The tops of the tables were fixed to the frame with wooden dowels, but in the 18th century, hand-made metal screws were used instead.

The turnings used on the legs and gateleg in pre-Restoration times favoured the ball turning and the bobbin turning, but later we find the *spiral twist* (or barley sugar twist) becoming popular. Eventually this was replaced by the *baluster* turning.

In post-Restoration times we also find tables made up in a size suitable for four or six diners, and a still larger version more likely to seat up to a dozen. Samuel Pepys records, "I found my new table very proper and will hold nine or ten people very well, but eight with great room". These tables abandoned the trestle leg principle as it was not strong enough with tables of great length, and the makers soon incorporated instead four turned legs on the fixed centre leaf. The larger tables also used two gates on each leaf to give more support. In a few cases, square gateleg tables are found, but often these prove to have been the central section of much larger sectional tables for banquet use. In these we find that the stretchers are turned, usually with a similar turning to that used on the legs and gate. The use of two gates on one side extended to small tables, as this gave firmer support for a writing surface which could be easily folded away, as the side table was designed to stand against a wall. The turned leg of the late 17th century, gave way in the 18th century to the cabriole leg, and in the late 18th century these terminated in a claw and ball foot.

CARD TABLES: 18th—19th Centuries

The 18th century saw an increase in the various types of tables in use, and most noticeable was the profusion of card tables. According to Percy Macquoid, a man of fashion at that period was "frequently passing half his day at cards and the remainder in drinking". This practice was not encouraged by Queen Anne, when a duty of 6d. was placed on each pack of cards and 5s. on each pair of dice. Queen Anne did not allow card playing in her presence. This puritan approach was not followed by her successors, for George II and Queen Caroline enjoyed regular gambling evenings at Court, and by 1786 Walpole was able to write "even the loss of £100,000 at cards was not rare enough to be surprising".

29

The features of these card tables include the introduction of the cabriole leg — taking over from the scroll-S leg. From 1712 onwards, many tables were designed as square, and these were firmly set on four legs, others had a folding top which relied for its support on a folding frame with wings in a concertina action. Also of note were the circular corners or dishes inset or bracketed at each corner to hold candlesticks and the frequent examples of wooden dishing inset into the surface of the table to hold the money or counters used by the card players.

The surface of the card tables was often covered with green baize but it might also be embroidered in a fine stitch with a pattern, scenes or designs incorporating a pack of cards.

Mahogany games table inlaid with several woods, c.1740.

Satinwood painted Pembroke table c.1790.

PEMBROKE TABLE: 1760—1830

Another prominent design among the smaller tables was the Pembroke. This is a small, lightly constructed table with falling leaves or end flaps, which are supported in position with *fly brackets* pivoted on self-hinges, and with the rule joint in use between the flaps and the fixed table top. A point which usually identifies a Pembroke table in comparison with sofa tables, is that the shape of the Pembroke when open is often rectangular or elliptical, instead of the longer shape of the sofa table.

This popular type of table was introduced in the 1760s, with George Kemp advertising it c.1760, and Chippendale including a table so described in a bill of

1766. The name is said to have come from "a Lady who first gave orders for one of them", possibly Lady Elizabeth who married the Tenth Earl of Pembroke in 1756, although John Gloag would opt for Herbert Henry, ninth Earl of Pembroke as its originator.

By the 1770s the Pembroke table was usually made of satinwood, incorporating marquetry, inlay and paintwork decoration. Sheraton included this type in his *Cabinet Dictionary* (1803) under the name of *Universal Table*, while in America, this type was used by Duncan Phyfe with lyre supports instead of legs c.1790-1800 in a design which has become a classic in reproduction furniture.

The supports of the Pembroke might also be of a curved X-shape, or, when the four legs were used, often square and tapered, linked together with a *saltire* (or diagonal cross) stretcher in which a small shelf was incorporated.

SOFA TABLE: 1780—1830

This was similar to the Pembroke, and might well be a development of it. The sofa table began to replace the Pembroke to some extent at the end of the 18th century. The table top was generally supported by two end supports or trestles, a single central pillar with outward curving feet, or with two pillar or scroll uprights linked at the base, which in turn has outward jutting feet with castors. It was popular in the late 1790s and Sheraton in his *Cabinet Dictionary* (1803) noted that the ladies "chiefly employ them to draw, write or read upon", and that they were used in front of sofas. They could be up to five feet in length extended, about 22ins to 24ins wide and about 28ins high. From 1810, sofa tables tend to be lower and smaller than these sizes.

Later models, which still use the name, varied in shape considerably. In some of them the drawer front would be a sham; in the early 19th century the table supports incorporated brass rods to symbolise cords. From c.1810, the sofa table was also supported on a single central pedestal which fitted into a square platform with four corner feet using brass inlays and brass claw feet. It was also designed with four turned spindles to replace the central pillar.

The lyre design used in the end supports c.1815 was replaced by 1820 with the open vase motif, and Therle Hughes suggests that by c.1825 the sofa table had lost its flaps and had little to distinguish it from other occasional tables, as this is the form in which George Smith illustrated it in 1826.

SPIDER LEG TABLES: 1760—1830

The gateleg tables continue to be made into the 19th century, but one form developed which was more in keeping with the elegant furniture of the late 18th century. This was the Spider Leg Table. These appear about 1760, and the name is due to the extreme slenderness of the turned legs, and the elegance of the narrow gates supporting the falling flaps, which tend to increase the width rather than the length of the table. It is possible that in some versions it may have had eight legs, as with the spider, and the legs are so slender that the inner leg of the gate was extended to the floor for extra support. The turnings of the legs and stretchers are left square where the joints appear, similar to the way in which the walnut Restoration chairs were made. The stretchers are sometimes inward curving to give more space for the user's legs. The term *spider* was in use in 1763 when Benjamin Goodison made a "mahogany spider-leg table with a drawer in it" for the Queen's House in St James's Park. In 1765 such a table was inventoried at *The Vyne* Hampshire. This type of table was identified in America when a "spider legge table £6" was made for Alexander Wright in November 1771 by Thomas Elfe of Charleston, South Carolina.

QUARTETTO TABLES: 1760—1840

With the advent of the second half of the 18th century, and the increase in types of tables, we find contemporary authors commenting on their increasing numbers in the house. John Byng in the *Torrington Diaries* complains about the "little skutting tables" he encountered, and the writer Maria Edgeworth (1767-1849) included some "small tables upon castors" among recent improvements which added to the comfort of the late 18th century home. Associated with tea-making, which was a new thing, were the nests of tables, very light, almost like trays with end supports which fitted one beneath the other. These were called *Quartetto tables* as there were usually four to a set, graduating in size which Sheraton termed "a kind of small table made to draw out of each other and again enclosed within each other when not in use". Such small tables could be used for needlework, or could be placed in the drawing room where, according to George Smith in *Household Furniture* (1808) they "prevent the company rising from their seats, when taking refreshments". When made in three these were called *trio tables,* and as four may also be called simply *quarto tables.* They are generally made with trestle ends incorporating two pillars set into a foot-bar with outward flaring scrollfeet. The slender legs have simple turnings while a curved stretcher at the back of each links the back pillars on each side. One variety has supports in the form of brass wires stretched diagonally linking the table top and feet. The tops are often veneered. A set made by Gillow c.1810 for Richard Gillow has bobbin type turnings, and four legs with side and back stretchers at three heights to strengthen the framework.

SIDE TABLES: 1600 onwards

The side table developed from the late 16th century examples of *hutch tables* with cupboards underneath which had in their turn evolved from the chest, and had by the 18th century in some instances become extravagantly carved and

17th century oak side table or serving table with drawer and decorated with lunette chip carving.

gilded pieces of furniture, with tops of marble or marquetry, to designs of Adam and others. These side tables fall into several types, and include the *pier tables*, which were designed to stand between windows against the pier or pillar, and *console tables* which are fixed to the wall and supported by front legs, but these are more of an architectural furniture than a typical piece of table furniture. Larger side tables were used in the dining room in the second half of the 18th century and were often made in pairs to stand one at each end of the room. The coming of the Restoration saw the introduction of walnut side tables c.1680 with scroll S shaped legs. These adopted bobbin or barley sugar twist turning later, and the cabriole leg appeared in the 1700s. This form of table grew in elaboration in the Queen Anne period, until about 1740, when the decoration became more restrained. By the 1760s the straight leg had come into favour, although it was at first somewhat heavy in form, made in sturdy square sections with fluting or fretted Gothic openwork. The 1790s exhibit more examples of

34

side tables with baluster legs, gilded or painted, while the different fashions of the 1790-1810 period produced elaborate examples of chinoiserie with leg supports made of gilt, and the use of Egyptian motifs recalls the wonders which followed Napoleon's progress through that campaign.

The tops of these tables were generally square in shape until the 1770s when semi-circular or semi-elliptical tops were designed. At the same time the serpentine shape came back into vogue.

The heavier tables were made with tops of inlaid marbles, Roman mosaic or painted wood, and the framework was of inlaid satinwood or carved and gilded pine.

The late 18th century saw a greater use of mahogany, with carved or inlaid work in various forms of decoration. The older tables topped with marble were by 1834 considered old fashioned, and the *Architectural Magazine* felt quite strongly that "Nobody will buy such pieces of furniture now".

The side table progressed in design to become the sideboard table on which silver plate was placed. Many similarities exist between the side table and the sideboard table in the 1760s to 1780s and so it is possible that the term was interchangeable.

PILLAR AND CLAW TABLES: 1700—1850

The introduction of tea into England from Holland took place in the early 17th century, but it wasn't until later in that century, that it became accessible and popular. The *Mercurius Politicus* (Sept. 23rd 1658) refers to "That excellent drink called by the Chinese Teka, by other nations Tay alias Tee". Pepys in 1667 notes that his wife is "making of tea, a drink which the Potticary (apothecary) tells her is good for her cold..." but it was not until 1679 that a reference to furniture connected with the beverage appears. This was when the Duchess of Lauderdale had 'a tea-table carved and gilt'.

The practice was at first limited to the rich, but in 1758 a pamphlet notes that "prevalent custom hath introduced it into every cottage and my gammer must have her tea twice a day". The early tea table c.1710 was made in walnut and was a simplified sidetable with cabriole legs, and this style with either the cabriole or later straighter leg of Gothic tracery c.1760 is to be found. A feature which separates it from the ordinary side-table is the gallery of tracery which is about 1½ inches high around the top of the table to stop the china sliding off. Contemporary with these, c.1730-1760, was the tea-table known as the *tripod*, the *claw*, or the *pillar and claw table*, often nowadays called the *pie-crust table*.

When Sir William Stanhope's house was sold in 1733, among the furniture was "a mahogany scallop'd tea-table on a claw". The size of the new mahogany timber made it possible to cut the round or octagonal table top from one piece of wood, and the surface was usually dished to give it a low sloping rim with a pie-crust motif. The shape of the table top varies from circular, serpentine, octagonal to octagonal-scalloped. The gallery, either in fretwork, or a rim supported by small spindles appeared in the 1750s. Tables of the 1740 to 1760 period were also made with eight dished circles or compartments around the scalloped edge which served to hold the cups or plates in position, and this was called a *supper table*.

The development of the legs is a useful dating factor, for the earlier examples retain the S-shape based on the cabriole leg, and they tend to ornament the curve of the knee. Late 18th century designs alter the shape to a slimmer, less curved shape. The actual foot is usually a club or pad foot, but the eagle's claw and ball was in use 1740-60, with the lion's paw in use in the 19th century. Additional to the richly carved mahogany tripod tables, much plainer oak tripod tables were made for use in inns, coffee-houses and tea-gardens. These probably had table tops made of joined timbers, and have not survived in the same numbers.

Mid-18th century pillar and claw table, with dished compartments to hold cups or plates.

In the first half of the 19th century the tops were plainer, but in the mid-Victorian period, they return to their more elaborate shapes. There were changes in the type of pillar supports. This was usually a turned baluster, but variants include the use of a fluted shaft with slender pillars around it, a shaft in a tripod form, or split into a tripod at the level where it meets the legs, while some late 18th century examples have no pillar, instead the tripod feet are carried up to the table top itself.

The next stage was to remove the tripod and replace it with a pedestal or plinth on castors or claw feet into which the turned and carved pedestal was mounted. In the late 1740s the table top was made so that it could be tilted sideways and so stand inconspicuously against a wall or in a corner. It was also made to swivel, and by 1755 some table tops could be removed and used as trays. For this a jointing system known as a *bird-cage* was introduced which, when the brass catch was released, enabled the table top to be tilted upright, and when the swivel wedge was removed, allowed the top to be taken away.

THE DRUM TABLE: 1760 onwards

The principle of the pillar and claw table was carried into the drum table, sometimes called the *rent table*, also a *monopodium*. This was a table top mounted on a heavy pillar and claw base. The circular top incorporated one or two rows of drawers or even sham drawers and bookshelves. It takes the name *rent table* because of its use in offices with the drawers labelled for the days of the week, so acting as a filing system for the rent collector or land agent. This type of table appeared in the late 1760s and was popular during the Regency period. They were built to stand firmly on four outward curved feet which sprang from a plain octagonal column supporting the heavy top. Thomas Hope designed a similar table with a triangular column which flairs out to three claw-foot terminals at the base — this he termed a monopodium, but they are also often called *library tables*.

3 Beds

When an inventory was made of the goods and furnishings of Cardinal Wolsey at Hampton Court Palace in the 16th century, the building contained two hundred and eighty beds! This is a measure of the richness of the Cardinal, and the height of luxury in which he and his retinue lived. For the earlier days of the medieval period we have very few examples of ancient beds previous to the 15th century, and so must rely heavily upon artists' impressions and the comments of contemporary writers.

It would appear that bedchambers were not the private — almost intimate rooms they had become by the late 19th century, and in general have remained into the 20th century. Instead, servants were used to going in and out freely, and guests were frequently received in them. The personal servants would sleep in the same rooms as their masters, and while the latter relaxed in the comfort of a flock mattress, the servants would lie on palliasses or the softest place which could be found on the rush covered floor. These palliasses, pallets or mats served as beds for the peasants too, and they could be easily laid on chests or in the box-like board beds which rested on the floor.

BOARDED BED AND THE BEDSTOCK: 14th—17th Centuries

The Saxon bed was known as the *shut bed* or *cabin bed* and was a kind of bunk or alcove which fitted into a wall. They could be two bunks high and a rough mattress lay on the wooden boards, with a curtain to draw right across the front for privacy. This mattress up to medieval times was a thin mat made of canvas or rush which in later days was laid below the feather-bed or down-bed used by the wealthier folk. In later Saxon periods a bed frame was introduced, initially a wooden platform on which the mat was placed. This developed into the *boarded bed* which was made like an open box with shallow sides and a straw or feather mattress lying on the boards which formed the bottom. These boarded beds were certainly in existence by the 14th century and these had spread to the labouring classes by the 16th century. The wealthier folk of the 12th to 14th centuries rested their feather beds on wooden boards raised off the ground on a wooden bedstead known as a *bedstock* or a *pair of bedstocks*. This was a framework made of four rails, joined to short posts at the corners which then formed the legs. In the early years of its existence these posts might be bobbin turned or faceted and could also be found surmounted with knobs.

38

Oak bedstead end, early 17th century.

The four low rails were drilled with holes through which cords could be threaded forming a loose network on to which the mattress of plaited rushes was placed. At a later date webbing was used, and this was known as *bottoming with girthwebb*. In the 12th century there is evidence of corner posts rising to 15 inches and low railing running round the four sides above the bed frame level. This served to contain the mattress or bedding, and it might also be broken on one side to enable the owner to get into bed with greater ease. The use of boards for the base of the *boarded bed* or the *bedstock* gave way to cords or webbing by the end of the 15th century. When this type of bed was used for servants, it was probably referred to in the inventories as a *livery bed,* and frequently listed in the servants' quarters.

STUMP BEDSTEADS, JOINED BEDSTEADS AND STANDING BEDS:
16th—19th Centuries

Next came the half-headed bedstead, more familiarly called the *stump bedstead* in which the wooden framework with four short turned or square legs was fitted with a plain head board. The term *stump bed* or *stumpend bedstead* is of 18th century origin. It was probably similar to the joined bedstead or standing bed of the 16th century inventories. This stump bedstead survived to the 1880s as such, and is also the basis of the 1920-30 simple wooden bed into which an iron mesh or spring base was fitted. John Loudon writes of them in 1839, "Stump beds are common in the humblest description of dwellings in England, both in town and country, they are commonly made of wood, with sacking bottoms, but as these articles are apt to harbour vermin, they have lately been manufactured entirely of woven iron; the place of the sacking or canvas bottom being supplied by interwoven iron hooping".

This mention of vermin highlights something which was an ever-present problem. As long ago as 1683 Thomas Tryon commented that "cleanliness in houses, expecially in beds, is a great preserver of health . . . beds which are often continued for several generations without changing the feather until the ticks be rotten". J. Southall wrote in 1730, "As Buggs have been known to be in England above sixty years, and every Season increasing so upon us, as to become terrible to almost every inhabitant . . .". To some people they were terrible trials; Lord Herbert writes in the 18th century, "What a night have I passed, not being able to get to sleep from animals crawling continually all over my poor dear person . . . though bugs do not like me in general". Others however took it in their stride; Samuel Pepys stopped at the '*George*' at Salisbury, "come about ten at night to a little inn, where were fain to go into a room where a pedlar was in bed, and made him rise, and there wife and I lay up, finding our bed good but lousy, which made us merry".

MATTRESSES

The mattresses were made of "thirteen pounds of carded wulle and covered with twelve elles of fyne hollands cloth" in the 16th century, while best mattresses were filled with swan's down, and the feather mattress was popular from the 14th century. Flock and wool were rather cheaper, in 1602 a flock mattress was valued at one to two shillings, and a feather mattress valued at thirteen to twenty-six shillings. Chaucer talks of "downe of pure dowres whyle, I will give him a fether bed..." Leaves were also used for stuffing mattresses. In 1664 Evelyn writes, "The leaves of the beech being gathered about the fall, and somewhat before they are frostbitten, afford the best and easiest mattresses in the world to lay under our quilts instead of straw".

The actual bedding consisted of a straw or wool pallet, two feather beds, sheets, blankets, another feather bed and overall an embroidered quilt. Sometimes this weight became excessive, (Wolsey had eight mattresses on his bed) and the height of the bedding often made it difficult to get into bed. Cost was another factor. Harrison comments "If it were so that our father had within seven years of his marriage purchased a matteress or a flocke bed... he thought himself to be as well lodged as the Lord of the town".

FIELD BEDS AND TRUSSING BEDS: 16th—19th Centuries

The practice of moving about from one house to another meant taking beds with them, and so special beds were made which could be dismantled easily, packed for carriage and quickly set up again. For this the frames were usually folding, and known by several names according to their type. There was firstly the *field bed*, noted in medieval inventories, but it would be wrong to consider them crude

Collapsable oak bed with wooden pins or screws holding the frame together, 17th century.

or uncomfortable. One made for the Earl of Leicester in about 1588 was "A felde bedsted of wallnuttree toppe fashion, the pillors and bedshead carved and garnished, pacell-gilte, my Lord's armes painted thereon. . . the celor and doble vallance of the same bed being of green velvet embroidered with narrow gards of green satin and purpled goulde. . . fyve curtains of green velvet", and so the description goes on. These field beds were also made for government use, the Treasury Warrant for 1729 included "four foure post field bedsteads of crimson harateen furniture, with complete sets of bedding". There was a necessity for such travelling beds as the beds in inns at home and abroad were not always clean.

Another type of travelling bed was called the *trussing bed*, a term used in the 15th and 16th centuries. The word itself meant the bed could be packed up and transported, and the lightweight framework was capable of being designed to hinge or fold into a very small space. Such beds still had cloth hangings above them, with curtains and draperies to suspend over the wooden framework.

The servants were not forgotten in the travels. In *'Northumberland Household Book'* we find "it is ordyned at every Removall that my Lords workmen in Householde as his Joner his Smyth and his Paynter with ij Mynstralles and also for the Carriage of V beddes viz, a bed for the Smyth, a bed for the Joner, a bed for the Paynter. . .".

TRUCKLE OR TRUNDLE BEDS: 14th—19th Centuries

Within the house itself for use by the servants were the *truckle, trundle* or *wheele beds*. Their use dates back to medieval times, and they were simple low bedstocks on wheels, which could be pushed out of sight under the main bedstead in the room during the day. They would be used for both servants and children, and were in use up to the 19th century. They went out of fashion to some extent in the late 16th and 17th centuries as the custom of servants sleeping with their masters declined and the introduction of nurseries came into fashion. Such beds were used under the Statutes of Corpus Christi College in the 15th century, where it was stipulated that the scholars should sleep in truckle beds below the Fellows — so presumably the Fellows used standing beds which were high off the ground.

THE HUNG BED OR FOUR POSTER: 12th—16th Centuries

The evolution of the bed from the low bedstock of Norman times developed in two ways. Firstly in the form of a simple bed as mentioned before, and secondly as a development which included the use of draperies around the bed. Curtains were at first hung on each side from horizontal rails which were attached to and projected from the walls in very much the same way in which they are used today to form a cubicle in a hospital ward. The curtains created small draught-proof rooms which gave privacy to the occupant. As the beds were often used as couches and seats during the day, these curtains could be drawn back or looped up out of the way.

In the 12th century there were examples where the curtains were hung between columns standing in the room, and by the 13th century there was a movement towards beds with a canopy, thus creating the *hanged* or *hung bed*.

The bedstead itself was, in the 12th to 13th century, still a rather ordinary piece of furniture, but as the medieval merchants and nobility sought to make their beds as rich-looking as possible, with the use of drapery, the woodwork itself was almost entirely hidden from view. The side curtains and the hanging over the bed were hung from the roof of the room by chains.

The terms used to describe the various parts of the bed date back to the 14th century. The light framework of wood supported from the ceiling on which the canopy draping rested was called the *tester*, from this was suspended at the head of the bed a backdrop of material called a *celour*. The *bed* itself was the mattress and bedding, whilst the wooden framework was known as the *bedstocks* or *bedstead*. It was common practice to have the curtains hung from the tester by rings, and the curtains would be hung up in the daytime in the form of a bag. In early days the canopy itself was a mark of honour, and consisted of either the whole tester extending over the whole bed, or the *half-tester* where the canopy only covered the half of the bed nearest to the bed-head or celour. There has often been confusion over the use of these terms, as the actual name of each part of the bed appears to have changed over the years. In medieval days it was possible to be aware of the degree of importance of a person by glancing at the furnishing of his bed. This becomes plain when reading the inventories:-

1412 Will of Roger Kyrkby, Vicar of Gainford . . . one bed in conformity with his position.

1382 Will of Joshua Mitford, widow, draper 'a bed embroidered, with demicelure', (here the use of demi-celure really means demi-tester or half-tester).

TENT BEDS: 15th—19th Centuries

While the rectangular tester was the common type of canopy in the middle ages, a *tent bed* was favoured in the 15th century. This had a round large ring, later called a *corona*, hanging high above the bed from which the draperies hung in the form of a bell tent. These were also called *Sparver beds*, and were in use in the 1440's when the Upholsterer's Company included them in their coat of arms. The sparver bed also appears in 16th century inventories:-

1504 a Rounde Sparver bed.

1526 A standing bed and a sparver like a tent.

43

These tent beds survived into the 18th century through designs of Sheraton and others and continued into the 19th century. J.C. Loudon in 1839 commented that "Tentbeds are in universal use, and scarcely require description".

The fact that not all the fine bedsteads were made for sleep is confirmed with the use of the *mourning bed*. Lord Verney had such a "great black bed that travels about the family whenever a death occurs". Sir Ralph Verney in the 17th century used to lend his out, and the widow would lie on it while receiving the

Victorian tent bed iron frame, made by Messrs. Peyton & Harlow of Birmingham.

condolences of her relatives and friends. At this time the duty of supplying a mourning bed and other sombre drapings was undertaken by the Upholsterer's Company, who were the recognised designers and makers of beds from at least 1360, when the formal government of the craft was documented.

They regulated all the textiles and materials which were used in the making of feather beds, bolsters, mattresses, cushions and quilts, and their ordinances forbad the use of deer's hair, goat's hair and fendown (cotton grass).

Beds were costly, and so precious that they were passed from father to son. Ralph, Lord Bassett, in his will of 1389, writes that he who "shall first bear my surname and arms, according to my will, shall have the use of my great velvet bed for life, but not to be alienated from him who should bear my name and arms...". In some instances these beds were even given names. The will of Richard, Earl of Arundel (1392) mentions a standing bed called *Clove,* while other beds are referred to by their material or colour, "to my daughter Charlton my bed of red silk, which is generally at Reigate; to my daughter Margaret my blue bed, usually at London".

The hung bed developed from the 13th to the 15th century, and even in the 16th century the remnants of privilege they evoked caused William Harrison in the 1580's to deplore that even the farmers "have learnt to garnish their joyned beds with tapestry and silk hangings".

SEALED BED OR FOUR POSTER: 16th—17th Centuries

Among the leaders of fashion in the 16th century, the wooden framework was taking on a new importance. In the opening years the wainscot head came into use, replacing the *celour* or draperies at the bed head, and a "sillow del waynscott" instead of the textiles is noted in the goods of Master Martin Colyns, Treasurer of York in 1508. This introduced also the more familiar of the older Tudor beds which we loosely call the *four-poster,* which is technically termed the *sealed bed* or by the term used in 1656, *posted bedstead.*

This new bed, which was of the late Tudor to Elizabethan era, had panelling seven to eight feet high at the head, and two *tail posts* at the foot. These tail posts might be fixed to the bedstead, or might even be separate posts, which with the head posts or wainscot celour supported a huge wooden canopy or tester which extended over the whole bed. The sealed bed formed a direct link with the built-in curtained alcove of Saxon days, and being constructed with a low flat tester, created the impression of a small sleeping chamber.

The change from the *hung bed* took place in the 15th century when the four posts took over the task of supporting the tester, and probably these at first still had drapery testers. Then the next stage in development was the wooden headpiece or *celour* fitted between the head posts, still covered with drapery, and finally the replacement of the canopy draperies with the wainscot tester. By

45

about 1550 the posts at the head of the bed were removed and the heavy tester was supported on the panelled and carved celour.

In the early years of the Elizabethan period, the sealed bed was confined to the wealthy, but within the next twenty-five years they had been brought to the home of the yeoman farmer.

In the early part of the Gothic period the bed posts were normally square or hexagonal in section with carved geometrical patterns. An early example was the bed of Henry III made in the 1240s, where the green posts were covered with gold stars "painted by Master William for 20 marks". Soon this elegance disappeared as the exuberance of the Elizabethan carving took over. After 1575 posts adopted the bulbous cap-and-cover motif, carved with gadrooning and acanthus leaves. Some late 17th century examples adopted architectural design, using fluted shafts topped with ionic capitals. The tail-posts were an integral part of the bedstead structure by 1600.

The Great Bed of Ware, late 16th century — 10ft. 8ins. square by 8ft. 9ins. high.

The tester or canopy was now made of wood and was panelled on the underface and decorated with a frieze of heavy moulding. The celour and other panels were often arcaded and motifs of flowers and goddesses were carved within them. The borders which ran along the frieze of the tester or enclosed the panels were incised runs of semi-circles infilled with smaller patterns or inlaid with different woods. When these beds had the curtains drawn, they were secure and warm, the owners had hiding places for valuables in the panelled head and small cupboards which might be used as shrines for the more religious, or a place for food for the night for the hungry. Above the level of the sleeper's head would be a ledge or shelf rail on which small articles and rushlights could be placed. These could be dangerous, Mrs Alice Thornton writes in 1661 "Nan Welburne haveing carelessly struck the candle at her bed head, and fell asleape, soe it fell downe on the pillow and on her head, and burned her clothes and being stifled by the smell it pleased God she awaked and put it out".

The carvings used in these beds changed their style by the 1650s becoming more formal and restrained, with some of the later oak work showing mitre work in the heavier panels. By the end of the 17th century the very heavy sealed beds with their wooden canopies were beginning to go out of fashion. The most famous example of the sealed bed can be seen in the Victoria and Albert Museum, which is the *Great Bed of Ware*. This was probably made for Sir Henry Fanshaw of Ware Park and was first referred to in 1596 in *Poetical Itinerary* of Prince Ludwig. By 1612 it was transferred to the White Hart and so moved from inn to inn in Ware until 1869 when it was removed to Rye House, Hoddeson. It is 10ft 8ins square and 8ft 9ins high, and on one occasion "six citizens and their wives came from London" and slept in the bed.

THE COVERED BED AND THE STATE BED: 17th—18th Centuries

While the sealed bed was popular from c.1500 to 1675 among the richer folk, the middle class and the yeomen, the *hung bed* was still a prestige item, and used for great occasions. It was no longer hung from the ceiling, so tended to be termed a *covered bed* as the woodwork supporting it was hidden and the draperies took precedence. In the early 17th century, upholstered beds of Italian style or design came into England, and after the Restoration of 1660, when Continental ideas and designs flooded into the country, the covered bed became established. In 1673 Evelyn noted that the Italians were discarding wood in favour of bedsteads of "forged iron gilded" which provided no crevises for parasites to breed in. The lofty rooms of the Stuart Period made the Elizabethan *sealed beds* of only seven to eight feet in height appear dwarfed, and new designs for State beds which towered to sixteen or eighteen feet were introduced. These were not for the normal house, and by no means all noble households had them. When George III and Queen Charlotte visited Wilton in 1779, the steward borrowed a "superb

State bed which we brought to Wilton, slung on the carriage of a waggon without the least damage, at no small expense, but when they arrived, they (George III) brought a snug double tent bed, had it put up . . . slept, for anything I know to the contrary, extremely quiet and well".

The height of these massive beds was exaggerated even more by the use of tall pinnacles or plumes on the four corner posts. The inventory of Hatfield Priory for 1626 included "i boxe with 8 feathers for ye beds" which refers to these plumes. The draperies of the bed which included a valance, tester curtains and quilt, were usually all made of the same material and it was quite proper for the walls of the room to be hung with panels of matching material called *costers*. The French fashion of the chairs and stools in the bedchamber matching the bed draping was introduced into England in about 1670.

Often these draperies were wildly extravagant, but for the more average member of the population, *fustian* or *steyned cloth* was used, and other materials for the still humbler bed would have included *worsted, dornix, counterfeit Baudekyn cloth* and *linen,* and "their beds are covered in tapestry, even those of the farmers".

The bedding for the rich was still swan's down, with a lower mattress of wool and dried vegetable substance known at that time as bastard down. The poorer occupants were used to bedding stuffed with animal hair, which was required by law to be cleaned for "if foul with grease it gives out by the heat of a man's body, a savour so abominable and contagious that many are destroyed thereby". The servants' beds were filled with chuff, leaves, straw, rush or fen-down. In the 17th century laths were fitted into the framework of the bedstead to replace the cords used previously, and this method became more general in the 18th century.

The mattresses were still piled high on the bed for comfort, and to enter the sheets a set of portable steps would be necessary, and by pulling a cord the curtains would draw, making a draught-proof, private compartment. The height of the bed was such as to remove the owner from the danger of rats and mice and in the richer households silver rat traps were an essential part of the gentleman's bedroom.

THE HALF-TESTER COVERED BED: 18th Century

The *half-tester,* in which the canopy covered a quarter to a third of the bed area, had been known in medieval days, and once again, in about 1700 it appears, sometimes linked to the name of the *angel bed* which seems to be much the same. In the 18th century mahogany gradually ousted walnut and oak as the chief timber used in fashionable households, and the cornice was freed of its fabric covering, and valances, and in the 1730s the foot posts and tail posts were revealed once again, showing a design of lighter, simpler classic lines. The height

Mahogany sealed bed c.1740 with fluted posts and Corinthian capitals.

of the beds in the 1720s was reduced, and the draperies on the celour were retained until about 1780, with the fabrics often glued in folds to the wood.

The bases of the new slender pillars were also uncovered, and in the 1720s the cabriole leg which had been introduced into chairs in about 1700 began to appear supporting the covered beds. The Chippendale designs of the 1750s used square posts on a plinth, and domed canopies appeared in use over beds and couches. The cornice of the tester became very simple in outline by 1775, either straight or serpentine, and often with graceful vase finials capping the four corner posts. We tend to forget that the four-poster was in fact a two poster with a panelled celour or headboard during the 15th to 18th centuries, and that it was in the 18th and 19th centuries that it became customary to flank the lower head board with posts to support the tester.

The posts themselves were made by bed-post turners, and a group of mahogany bed-post turners would prepare designs which they then submitted to the *upholders* or bedmakers, for incorporation in their bed design. Most posts would be 8ft in length, and others, those for the State Beds, could be almost twice as long but made in parts and fitted together. The mahogany used up to the 1750s was the hard San Domingo variety, but when in the 1740s the Honduras mahogany became available the turning was greatly speeded up. Bed-posts were often made in four sections, the feet, the lower baluster section, the upper section and the tapering cornice peg with the whole joined by dowels.

As the great designers of the 18th century applied themselves to bed design, so the characteristics of each emerges. Chippendale used low relief carving, and employed the lion's paw for the lower section of the post. His bedstead in Chinese style in the Victoria and Albert Museum is extremely fanciful, and he was fond of cluster-column bedposts. When posts were ebonised or gilded, the turning could be carved out of soft wood such as beech, which when gilded gave a rich effect without the cost of using more expensive woods.

The *cornices* which are used to edge the tester, were made by the cornice-maker, who was a carver, often making window cornices to match the bed cornice design. The heavier cornices of the earlier beds were made much narrower from about 1780, and were shaped in straight, bowed or serpentine outline. Frequently to meet the demands of specialised work in the style of Chinoiserie, Gothic or French furniture,, decoration such as pineapples, dragons or palm trees occur, which have to be transferred into wood and then gilded, giving a very exotic effect.

A restraining influence appeared in the 1760s due to Robert Adams' classical training, and Hepplewhite also placed his mark on bed design, using shapely reeded or fluted posts with slender urn-shape swelling and carved twists of ribbon or flowers which spiral down the posts. Sheraton, however, leaned towards the exhuberant, producing designs with massed looping of draperies, domes rising high in the rooms, topped with crowns, plumes or pineapples. In

Chippendale bed in Chinese style, japanned black and gold with scrolled finials on the cornice which support gilt dragons, c.1755.

Mid-17th century box bed in wainscott with incised carving.

fact one contemporary writer comments "grace was sacrificed for weight once again".

About the second half of the 18th century the designer's influence gave place to the shopkeeper-manufacturer, who often sought novelty to attract customers and draw them away from competitors. The four poster was not entirely abandoned, but the half tester became more popular, usually made of carved mahogany with curtains hung around the head so that the bed did not appear to protrude so prominently into the bedroom. The vogue for metal fittings and decoration which embellished the Regency and early Victorian beds spread to the use of metal and brass in making the beds themselves, so that by the Great Exhibition of 1851 the brass bedstead became most fashionable. They were made with full or half-testers, also as a camp bed with a canopy or a tent-like dome which harked back to the designs of the late 18th century.

The supporting laths used in the 18th century and early years of the 19th century to support the mattress, gave way to the use of metal mesh in a wide diamond pattern. When John Loudon described the cottage furniture of the 1830s he was able to comment on the use of half-testers for "use in small rooms, where it may be desirable to turn them up during the day" implying that they folded back against the bed head. He also noted that "stump bedsteads are common in the humblest description of dwellings in England, and tent beds which are in universal use".

Among the many types of beds which proliferated in the 19th century were two which in their origins take us back to the 16th century. First was the *box bed* which was a refinement of the Saxon *shut bed,* a bedstead enclosed on two or three sides by framed panelling having a flat tester over the top and curtains to draw across the opening. These were very solid items of furniture which were matched to the wainscotting of the panelled room and so required no additionl ornament other than a simple curtain on one side. Robert Loudon, writing in the 1830s, does not like them, but adds that "there is generally a shelf, and sometimes two, fixed to the inside of the bottom of the bed; so that this piece of furniture not only serves as a bed, but as a wardrobe and linen chest". Sometimes the curtain was replaced by bed-doors fixed in position with bolts.

The other bed of interest was the *press bedstead* which appears to be a development of the trussing bed. These folded up into cupboards or mock chests of drawers. Loudon also states that they "are very common in kitchens... but they are objectionable as harbouring vermin... they have however one advantage, which is, that persons sleeping in them are generally obliged to get up betimes in the morning". Oliver Goldsmith in his 'Deserted Village' (1770) points out to us that :-

> The chest contrived a double debt to pay,
> A bed by night and chest of drawers by day.

4 The Chest, Chest of Drawers and Dressing Table

The chest was one of the very basic pieces of early furniture, and it is the only item of medieval furnishing to survive in any quantity. In the sparsely furnished houses of the 10th and 11th centuries chests were used for many purposes. They were used as receptacles for books, clothes, sometimes for silver plate, personal effects and even treasures which could be kept safe within their strengthened sides. Special chests were made for the King's Household, and certain of these, made to contain particular documents, are named after the manuscripts they have protected. Today at the Public Record Office can be seen the Domesday Book of 1086 in the *'Domesday Chest'* or the *'Treaty of Calais Chest'* which was made c.1360.

The normal family chests, being of reasonable size, were always ready to be moved with the household at a moment's notice, or even taken away and hidden in times of danger. In some instances chests were used by the Church to guard the precious relics of the Saints, and when the tomb of St Cuthbert was opened in 1104, the body was contained in an outer chest of leather with iron nails and clasps, within a second inner chest of carved oak, and in a third innermost chest studded with gold and jewels. In 1166 Henry II commanded that 'trunks' be placed in each church in order that the congregation could pay their share towards the cost of the Crusades. In the same way the 'Chronicle' of Jocelin of Brakelond (written c.1173) recorded that the keeper of the Shrine of St Edmund should make a certain hollow trunk with a hole in the lid, fastened with an iron lock, "so that therein persons might put their contributions for the building of the tower".

In Anglo-Saxon times the coffer was called a *loc,* hence the modern word *locker,* or it might also be called a *cyste,* which word gave rise to the more well known term *chest.* French-Norman use produced the other terms *hutche* and *coffre* which in turn were anglicised to become *hutch* and *coffer.*

These two main types of container (the chest and the coffer) existed side by side, and their basic difference was explained by Randle Holme in *'Academy of Armour'* (manuscript dated 1649) which states that "if it have a straight and flat cover, is called a chest, which in all other things represent the coffer save in the want of a circular lid or cover" or basically that a chest has a flat lid, while a coffer boasts a coved lid! Unfortunately neither the development of this type of furniture, nor the writers of its history agree on so simple a definition.

Ralph Edwards puts it another way, "a chest is a receptacle of wood made by a

Chest used as a counter in this 15th century illustration.

carpenter or joiner, while a coffer is reserved for travelling chests (also called trunks) and for coved or canted lid receptacles". More recently Penelope Eames divides them into hutches with legs and chests without, so the situation is confused. If the historic development and use is taken into consideration, some order emerges. The North country word *arc* was used in medieval times and applied to chests used for the storage of flour, meal and bread. In East Anglia the term *hutch* is used and applied to a chest with legs which preserved the contents from the damp floors and unclean surfaces.

THE COFFER

The coffer usually had handles, a domed or canted lid and no feet. They were made for travelling, and were also known as *trussing coffers, sumpter chests,* and in a much larger form as *standards.* These coffers were carried in waggons or hung in pairs across the backs of horses, known as *sumpter horses.* Having no legs or projections, they created less problems in carriage. Occasionally a protective

55

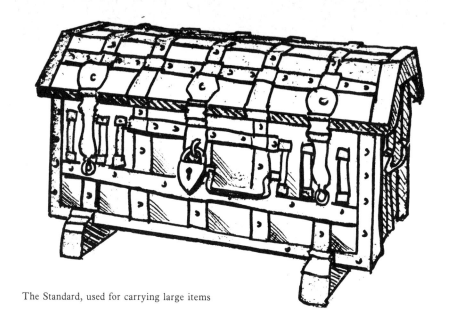

The Standard, used for carrying large items

covering called a *bahut* was used, made of tapestry, or where valuables or other contents were susceptible to damp, these bahuts may be made of wood or leather and act as an outer chest or covering. The coved lid was made to throw off the rain, and as it was closed with a flanged joint, it reduced even more the danger of dampness to the contents. In the 13th century these trussing coffers were lightweight wooden cases, and the protection against the elements was provided by a cover of leather, oxhide, or the more expensive Russian leather. The leather used was known as *cuir buoilli*, which was hide treated with oil until it was easily worked and almost impervious to rain. If the chests were to be carried under cover, such as in a *bahut*, they were upholstered with velvet *fustian* from Naples, silk or other rich fabrics, and perhaps also trimmed with cut-fringes. The leather itself was sometimes painted or gilded — particularly with imported coffers from Spain or Holland, and ornament and initials could be added by the use of close studding the brass headed nails which secured the leather or cloth to the inner wooden container.

These coffers were not always large, being intended for the transport of smaller objects, while for wholesale work the *standard* was used. This was a much larger chest, bound in iron, and referred to as a *standard* in 15th century inventories. Such *standards* were used for packing and storing goods in much the same way as the large container boxes are used for house removals today. Like the trussing coffers they had domed or gabled lids and were covered in leather or cloth. Their contents would be wrapped in cloth and the *standards* were usually carried in carts.

The man who made such travelling chests was known as the *Cofferer*, and the Guild of Cofferers had records dating back to the early 14th century, when in 1328, Salamon le Coffrer was elected to the Guild to undertake "the Mystery's government and instruction".

DUG-OUT CHESTS: 900—1300

The use of chests in pre-Norman times has been assumed from comments in Anglo-Saxon laws which expected the Lady of the Household to remember her "duty to keep the keys of them, namely her storehouse, and her chest and her box". Such chests were kept in the chamber, being the most secure part of the house, and often stood side by side, or at the foot of the bed. In this position they could be used as a seat by day and a bed for a servant or page at night.

Lidded storage furniture such as these chests stemmed from the ancient hollowed trunk called the *dug-out*, known well before the time of the Conquest. They are referred to in older documents as *trunks* and this name must surely have come from the tree-trunks from which they were shaped. The round outside shape of the trunk was levelled with an adze on the base to make it stand level on the floor, and it was then hollowed, and either had the sawn-off top fitted to form the lid (often split into two lids) or a rough plank lid added. Such trunks were most useful as collecting boxes as their great weight made them difficult to move and the small hollowed-out space was quite adequate for this purpose. Such boxes were in use up to the 14th century.

The value of the money collected in these chests, or the plate of valuables likely to be stored in them caused them to be banded with iron for security, and in some instance the whole chest was criss-crossed with iron bands and intricate locks, so they became the early *strong-boxes* or *safes* with which we are familiar today. The use of several locks did not only mean greater overall security, it usually denoted a shared responsibility for its safety. The Common Chest of the London Guildhall, made c.1427, had six locks with the keys held by designated officers, and the London Merchant, John Coventre, left four keys to his plate chest on his death, one for each executor, to ensure the valuables were safe from any one of them.

THE BOARDED CHEST

The chest proper seems to have evolved through five main constructional forms commencing with the basic dug-out form of about 900-1300 AD. The next stage is called the *boarded chest* and this was made of *slab construction*. It consisted of six heavy boards or planks, often roughly adzed, which were pegged together at the ends, each showing a flush surface, and each plank forming either the side, the top or base of the chest. Early examples, called an *arc*, were constructed with

Oak boarded chest, late 15th century.

sides raised at the back, into which the lid was hinged on wooden pegs, so forming a pivot. By the end of the 13th century, metal strap hinges made by the blacksmith were added, and from early Tudor times the planks or boards were smoothed or faced with an adze.

JOINED CHESTS: 1250—1500

As the demand for chests grew, the craftsman concentrated on its production and his technique improved. Legs appeared by extending the sides below the level of the chest, forming the basis of the later *hutch* design. In time the sides, formerly heavy planks, were made thinner, and at the next stage, four heavy vertical timbers called *stiles,* were fitted to each corner, into which the sides of the chest tongued into long grooves cut into the *stiles* and were then pegged into position. This formed the *joined chest* . This gave a stronger construction, which did not depend so heavily on the metal banding for security, so in its place came more attractive surface decoration, often in the form of *chip-carving.* The

58

patterns often in the form of rosettes, were usually geometrical, as they could be marked out with a compass and then chipped out of the surface of the wood after the pattern had been incised with a sharp knife or chisel. This simple incised decoration, which appears in the period c.1550-1660, was usually done by the maker of the chest, rather than a qualified woodcarver, and at the same time, the heavy iron nails found in the medieval chest, gave way to smaller nails and wooden pegs for jointing.

Within the chest itself was often a little trough or box, which are called *tills*, a word still in use in shops for holding cash. They may have been used for

Oak chest or arc with canted lid revolving on a horizontal pivot, 15th century.

valuables, but could also have held fragrant herbs to keep the contents of the chest sweet. The boarded chest continued to be made for many years, even into the 18th century. But the late 15th century, the elaborate use of iron had disappeared.

The timbers used in making chests and coffers included oak, walnut, chestnut, elm and fir. Another wood introduced in the early 16th century was cypress, used as a precaution against moths. The chests of cypress were heavily taxed under the 1689 *Act of Tonnage and Poundage.* Cedar was popular for blanket chests, and these were often imported from Holland, while in the 18th century, the more elaborate mule chest was lined with the fragrant cedar wood.

The planks used in making chests were still not always sawn, but split with a *riving knife* or *froe,* as such cleft boards were very strong. In the 17th century the boards were uniformly ⅝ins to ¾ins in width, which helped to make the chests light and neat. The size of the chests became smaller, ranging from two feet to five feet in length.

The term *joined* or *joyned,* which was applied to this stage of development, was also applied to chairs, stools, tables and forms, and it appears in inventories in the 15th century, and seems to distinguish the items made by the joiner, from those made by the carpenter without the use of joints.

FRAMED OR PANELLED CHESTS: 1400 onwards

In Norman times, the woodwork was split between the shipwright, the carpenter and the wheelwright, but as the house and its contents became more

Oak framed or panelled chest, mid 17th Century, painted in reds and greens with tulips and carnations in vases.

Linen fold panelled chest, Mid-16th Century.

elaborate, separate craftsmen appeared. The carpenter relied on the strength of his work from its sheer size, bulk and postition, which with the use of nails or pegs, made them secure. The joiner, however, depended much more on the firmness and accuracy of his joints to achieve the same result. In the next stage of the development of the chest, this point is illustrated, for the heavy oak stiles of the joined chest are exchanged for more slender squared timbers into which the rails were tenoned, and so the new type of chest was known as *framed* or panelled.

The term *tenon* comes from the French word *tenir,* which means 'to hold', and this joint allowed the use of a framework which was linked by mortise and tenon joints with the *stiles, muntins* and *rails* enclosing loose panels. The lid was made of flat boards joined underside with cross battens, becoming thinner at the start of the 17th century, and by the 1620s panelled tops appeared.

Such panels were initially plain, the method of framing was introduced from Flanders about 1400-1450. A very early example of panelling in England is in the sides of the chest in the Chapel of the Pyx, Westminster Abbey, dated c.1482. The use of the familiar *linenfold* design is to be found in the late 15th century and was brought into use in England c.1498-1524, while the *parchment* or *parchemin* panel came in the early 16th century. Panelled construction was virtually ignored in England until the 15th century, with heavy panelling being

61

introduced into chests c.1500 and light panelling not in use to any great extent before the 1530s.

The influence on the native English designs of the Continental workers was great. This was not only due to the close Continental relationship of those days, owing to political and religious links, but also because of the large importation of both timbers and finished pieces of furniture into this country. Included in the will of John de Coggeshale, a London Corder, dated 1384, was "a great chest of Gascony" while the largest number of foreign imports relates to Flanders chests. In 1483 the Guild of Cofferers was so worried at the stream of furniture arriving from Flanders, that they petitioned Richard III, as they felt that they were "like to be undone by the said wares". A statute prohibited these imports, but after Richard's death the flow resumed with coffers of spruce and deal coming into this country from the Baltic ports, in particular Danzig from which the Dansk chests are named. These Dansk chests are to be found in inventories of the 15th and 16th centuries, while chests of cypress were coming in from Italy. In some instances the chests were imported in groups of three, each fitting inside each other.

The decoration on the chests increased in artistic craftsmanship; Renaissance portraits in square panels and other Italian style motifs such as *roundels* began to influence the more native Gothic traditions by about the 1530s. By the time of the Wars of the Roses (1455-85) the use of the *mitre* became popular in England, and the medieval passion for colour and gilding was extended to many of the earlier chests. The will of John Somersham, dated 1368 mentions particularly his "painted chest of Flemish work", and while this practice lingered on in the painting of the interior of chests into the 18th century, it was the exterior carving of the panels and stiles which recalls the glory of the 16th and 17th century examples.

Even in this period, the English chest never seemed to achieve the wealth of decoration found on some Continental chests. In particular, it is noticeable that only the front was carved, while the lid, sides and back were seldom so richly ornamented. The presence of so many foreign chests in this country is also an interesting thought, for besides those imported under normal practice, many were brought to this country by travellers such as clergy and diplomats who were resident for some time in foreign parts, and who needed containers to bring their goods back to their homeland.

In the late 17th century, at the time of the Restoration, we find that walnut was in vogue and elaborate examples of walnut chests were imported from the East. Samuel Pepys visited the Duke of York in 1661; he was very impressed with "two very fine chests covered with gold and Indian varnish given him by the East India Company of Holland".

As chests became more elaborately patterned, so their nature and use gradually changed. From the middle of the 16th century, some chests and travelling coffers

62

were fitted with small drawers or *tills,* and these were called *drawer boxes* in the inventories. In the joined chest, the inclusion of the drawer was no innovation, as it had already started on the Continent, and as early as the 1580s Hugh Offley's chest in Southwark Cathedral had three drawers in the lower part.

MULE CHESTS: 17th Century

In general, however, chests were used for clothes, but this method of storage had its difficulties, as it was inconvenient for the storing of smaller items of clothing. So by about 1650 a hybrid form, half cabinet, half chest of drawers came into use. At first smaller drawers were enclosed behind cupboard doors, and the fronts were often elaborately inlaid and panelled. Evelyn refers to chests with drawers in his diary in 1679. The design with a lifting top disclosing a well beneath is most useful, and by the end of Charles II's reign the last reminder that the chest of drawers had evolved from the chest had disappeared.

The original 14th century use of low legs formed from the wide stiles of the chest, was carefully changed to the more acceptable bracket or bun feet fitted to the bottom of the chest c.1680-95. The chests were even raised on low stands of about one foot in height, and the chest itself again fitted with brass handles on each side to allow it to be lifted off the stands. The advantage of raising the lower drawers from the floor brought in stands with baluster or spiral turned legs. The early drawers were often crudely made, pinned together until the time when the joiner began dovetailing the front and sides in the mid to late 17th century. The bottom boards of the drawers were nailed, and by the first half of the 17th century this type of chest, which appears in the inventories as a *drawerchest* also became known as the *mule chest.* Gradually the chest areas were reduced by the drawers until the *chest of drawers* appeared in inventories of the 1670s under that name.

TALLBOYS, CHESTS & DRAWERS: 17th Century onwards

In 1700, tallboys, or double chests of drawers were introduced, and so we find the lower stand of the chest replaced by drawers, and the upper section making the piece rise to six feet in height, containing up to five or six full drawers and several smaller half width drawers. With the earlier chests, wooden knobs are present, but these were replaced by brass pulls and escutcheons and between 1670 and 1700 the brass handles change from pendant knobs to loops or rings, and then to loops with back-plates. The tallboys were topped by a curved or broken pediment, or a straight hollow cornice. A pull-out surface slides from the centre division at table height, and the original applied decoration of the mule chests and chests of drawers is on occasions replaced by walnut burr veneer to great advantage. These tall pieces were usually confined to the living room.

Chest of drawers with brass escutcheon plates and drop handles, late 17th century.

Dressing commode of mahogany inlaid with satinwood c.1780.

The chest of drawers on a stand persisted in popularity, but the earlier baluster legs gave way to the fashionable cabriole shape, and like the evolution on the legs of chairs and tables, gradually changed from the early narrow *shoulder* or *knees* to the heavier form with shell or acanthus leaf carving crisply cut. Later tallboys incorporated the swan-neck pediment and late into the 18th century the design of the chest of drawers and the tallboy became more severe, often made of plain mahogany on a base or carcase of pine with oak used in the drawer linings. Serpentine and serpentine-breakfronted chests were designed in the 1760s and the familiar bow fronted chest of drawers made for the bedroom appeared about 1800, with smarter examples frequently incorporating vertical turned pillars at the front corners.

The construction of the serpentine curve involved the task of ensuring that the

65

Gentleman's elaborate travelling dressing table c.1810, with carrying handles.

drawer fronts retained their shape. These were made from pieces of deal, mahogany and oak, built up and glued into shape, and once the drawer was rigid it was veneered with mahogany or a wood-facing.

THE COMMODE: 18th—19th Centuries

During the second half of the 18th century, the chest of drawers was over-shadowed by the *commode*, which was not, as is commonly considered, a closet chair, but a term used by Thomas Chippendale to cover such a variety of items of furniture that the inclusion of drawers alone seems to have been sufficient cause for this name to be applied. The popularity of the French fashion at the time of the publication of Chippendale's *'Director'* probably explains his preferences for the commode, and the French influence is quite noticeable. Other makers such as Ince and Mayhew, or Benjamin Goodison in 1758, compromised by calling the item a "mahogany commode chest of drawers". However the original French commode from which the designs were taken was originally a low armoire with drawers, which, by the time of the accession of Louis XV had taken on the curved shape and exhuberant ornament with which it is usually associated. In the 18th century the *'French commode'* was a desirable and prominent item, and no fashionable drawing room was complete without one. Chippendale made commode-tables, and commode-clothes presses, and really the separation between the English chest of drawers and the French style commode lies almost entirely on the degree of gallic element in the design.

The basic shape falls into three main outlines. Firstly the early Chippendale influenced styles with a *bombe* element in the side elevation; then the more square vertical shape with the *serpentine* front which Chippendale highlights in the 1770s; thirdly the familiar Adam style half-round commode of the 1770s-1780s.

The fittings of the chests are often a guide to their age, but must be used with caution. The plain brass keyhole fittings were originally cast and are straight at the bottom narrow end. Later or modern copies tend to be shaped by machine and so have more curve in the outline. The dust moulding, which is the quarter-round should be evident in the drawers, but it is unlikely to be found prior to the early 18th century.

DRESSING TABLES: 18th Century onwards

Early chests with lifting tops were re-introduced in the late 18th century as *dressing chests.* These appear in Thomas Shearer's designs, exhibiting a top-drawer which had compartments for toilet items, and a mirror which could be raised in a stand. This lifting top was also used by Chippendale and Sheraton, with a bowl fitted in front of the mirror shown in a design of 1803. It would however be wrong to attribute the use of these dressing tables or dressing chests to the women alone, for it was not unknown for men to spend considerable time and money on their appearances. In 1548 Bishop John Hooper complained that the "forty shillings a year a man will waste on his morning times while he sets his beard in order", and later in 1583 Philip Stubbs writing in his *'Anatomie of abuses'* complains that English women were not content with their faces, but must "adulterate the Lord's workmanship with unguents and cosmetics".

The many bottles, preparations, brushes and combs were at first laid out on tables, but before long a casket containing small drawers, but with a drop-down front on two cupboard doors, became essential to the Elizabethan and Stuart lady. Those made of wood, were often covered with embroidery, and in the early Stuart period the stump-work cabinets and caskets were particularly attractive. In time these caskets were raised on legs and by 1652 special furniture was appearing for toilet use. An inventory of that date of Derham Hall includes "one dressing table and stand" and by the 1730s such tables had been fitted with a kneehole, drawers on each side, and a lift-up top under which the mirror and cosmetic boxes were arranged.

These mid-18th century dressing tables resemble the bureau or writing desks of the same period, and were often made as a dual piece of furniture, having a pull-out writing surface and a drawer fitted with writing materials. Just as one type of dressing table emulated the chest of drawers or bureau, the other type was created by the addition of fabrics to make it more of a bedroom or dressing-room item. At first the table tops were protected by deeply fringed drapery, and in time the mirror was added as a fixture on the top, sometimes with candlesticks attached. By the 1730s further drapery called *petticoats* hung in swathes draped across the legs, made of damask, or in the 1760s lighter fabrics to match the other furnishings in the rooms.

5 Cupboards, Dressers and Wardrobes

The changing names of pieces of furniture over the centuries have always caused confusion, but the situation is nowhere so difficult as with the early types of cupboard. The leading authorities frequently differ as to which label to use, so here I have attempted to follow a use of names which does not conflict with historical use.

CUPBOARDS

We know that the cupboard was in use and was a reasonably common piece of furniture before the time of Queen Elizabeth I, but the form of such a cupboard was, as the name implies, a board or shelf for the display and service of cups and plates. The easiest description of this type of cupboard is given in Sir Thomas Kyton's inventory of 1603:-

Item, a thing like stayres to set plate on

In the nobleman's hall these tall stepped units with a series of open display shelves were most important, for like the chair and the bed, it was possible to discern the degree of honour or estate of the owner by the number of shelves it displayed. In France, where the nobility took these things seriously, Alienor de Poitiers recommends:-

The Queen of France — five shelves
Isabella of Portugal — four shelves
Countesses — three shelves
Wives of bannerets — two shelves
Less noble women — one shelf

In England, when Henry VII held a banquet at Richmond, his *buffet,* as this unit was called, rose to nine or ten stages. So an item which started off in the 12th or 13th century as a cupboard was, by the 15th century, an important way of showing your station and wealth in society. This *cupboard* or *buffet* was covered with draperies or pieces of carpet when in use, and a portable type which had no back or canopy, was made in a form which could be taken apart for travelling.

Cardinal Wolsey, who was not noted for his modesty, enjoyed at Hampton Court a "cup-board... of six desks high full of gilt plate, very sumptious". Generally this form of display was not considered ostentatious, rather, it was a

69

gesture made to welcome and honour the invited guest. Such a display can still be seen at the Guildhall on State occasions.

The *buffet* was also used in the hall or chamber as a form of sideboard for serving the wine when important guests were present. In extremely rich examples the buffet is high, well carved in Gothic style and fitted with an architecturally designed canopy. In case it should be thought that this type of furniture was too fine for the normal household, Harrison notes that while the nobleman had "so much plate as may furnish sundry cupboards" it was as obvious that the farmer had "a fair garnish of pewter on his cupboard" and for the poorer household the *pottshelfe* was always possible.

While the buffet was a cupboard used for display, the *dressoir* was used in the servants' quarters and in the service area of the hall for the storage of dishes and utensils, acting as food counters and hatches to halls and chambers. As such, it did not follow the pattern of the buffet in using a required number of shelves. In fact, Penelope Eames notes that the main way of identifying the buffet and the dressoir in inventories, lies in the part of the house in which they are listed. The buffet is in the hall and chamber, while the dressoir is in the servants' rooms. Donald Smith links the famous Yeoman of the Guard to the buffet, and the Tudor servant was the buffetier who tended the buffet, which over the years was changed to the *beefeater*, a definition, however, which is not wholly accepted.

THE ARMOIRE AND AUMBRY: 1300—1550

In the medieval period the *armoire* or *aumbry* was the equivalent of the modern cupboard. It became part of the fabric of the building, in the form of wall cupboards set into the stone walls of castles and churches, but in the later Middle Ages, free standing armoires developed. These at first were simple box-like structures with shelves and doors. It is this fact of the *door* which made the difference between the buffet and armoire. The goods in Botolf Lane in London in 1485 included "in the chambre by the Sommer parlour "... a grete new standing almerye with ij levys... in the kechen a great almarye with ij leves..." (in the kitchen a great armoire with two leaves).

Armoires were used for clothes to a great extent:-

> *"1256 To Godfrey de Lyston... to make an almariolum in the
> middle of the turret in the upper bailey to keep the
> Queen's clothes"*

They were also used for the storage of records, books, chapel ornaments and vestments, and also for the storage of food and utensils.

> *"1391 Inventory of the goods of Richard Toky, grocer. Pantry
> and Buttery. One ambry 40d. and one hanging ambry..."*

The French use of armoire has survived to this day, but in England, in early days, the term had change to aumbry, ambry and almery. The *almery* also

The aumbry or oak standing cupboard, the panels pierced and carved with tracery and symbols of 'A' and feathers c.1500, possibly linked to Arthur, Prince of Wales.

evolved from the *hutch*, which was a kind of box in which the broken meats and bread from the table were stored before being given to the poor as alms.

During the second half of the 15th century, cupboards *with* aumbries appear in the inventories, and around the reign of Henry VIII the modern meaning of cupboard was given to what had previously been called the aumbry. It seems that they were frequently used for food. John Smythe of Blackmore Priory refers in his will of 1543 to "a fyne almery with four dores for breade", while somewhat earlier in 1373 the inventory of Thomas Mockyng, fishmonger of London, shows that he had "two ambries for food, three chests for cloths and one board for cups called a cupboard".

The term aumbry not only meant a free-standing cupboard, but also a small enclosed cupboard contained in the structure of other furniture. So in 1485 we read of "an almery wt a cupboard above it" meaning a cupboard with a display shelf above, while in 1527 "a wayn scott cupboard wt too aumbries" meant a panelled display unit with two enclosed cupboards with doors. When Cardinal Wolsey's possessions were listed in 1527 there were twenty-one "cupboardes of waynescotte whereof V be close cupboards" i.e. with doors.

About this time, in the 16th century, there was a change in dining habits, with the master of the house and his immediate family using a dining room or private chamber instead of the main hall. This started between 1330-1400, as William Langland in writing *Piers Plowman* (1362) pointed out, the rich no longer lived with their servants as of old, but instead ate "in a privy parlour with a chimney". Private dining parlours as such were not common until the 16th century. At this time storage cupboards with doors were being developed for different purposes, and were conforming to more recognised patterns.

COURT CUPBOARDS: 1500—1700

The court cupboard is the most familiar, and is the direct descendant of the buffet or the true cup-board. It consists of a lower *pottshelfe* just off the floor, and two heavy shelves or *stages* for the display of cups and plate. The name may have been taken from the French word *court* which means short. They are rarely more than four feet high, being rather lower than the *presses* or *press-cup-boards* which followed them. Like the earlier buffet they were frequently used for display. In 1606 there is a reference to "my courte cupboard with its furniture of plate". An early illustration of the court cupboard is shown in Holbein's painting of *'The Ambassadors'* (1533). In an inventory in 1552 of Paget Place, St. Clements Dane, they are listed in secondary bedchambers, indicating that at that time they were sufficiently old as to warrant being relegated to less well furnished rooms. Also they were probably no longer used for plate, but more likely to hold washing utensils or even overnight food.

So the standard design we know today must have been common in the 1550s, for as early as 1575 two court cupboards in the Great Chamber of Lambeth Palace were described as already 'olde'. They could be dismantled into two or more parts when necessary, and in Shakespeare's Romeo and Juliet are the lines:-

> *"Away with the joint-stools, remove the court cupboards,*
> *Look to the plate"*

The three stages or tiers of open shelving had deeply carved friezes. The shelves were held in position by dowel pegs, and they had moulded edges. The central stage often had bold gadrooning, while in the lower stages a chequer pattern in different woods might be used.

Drawers were incorporated in the frieze of the middle and top stages, which pulled out on grooved runners, but they were not obvious, being carved to make the frieze appear one piece. When handles and knobs appear on 16th century court cupboards, they are generally later additions. These drawers were probably used for storing knives and spoons; forks were not yet commonly used. The

72

contents were apparently considered valuable, as in 1596 Sir Frances Carew of Beddington had "a court cubberd with two drawers and locks to them".

The back support posts were square sectioned with simple repetitive carving such as chevrons or gadrooning, and where feet were added, they would be plain square or bun-shape. But the chief features of the court cupboards were the bulbous columns which separated the heavy open shelves. Early examples show the columns with acorns and deeply carved foliage and flowers, combined with voluted caps, while the early 17th century examples have more elongated pear-shaped bulbs, and in the mid 17th century they had lost their lavish carving and more resembled baluster leg turnings.

In some richer examples, there is great emphasis on the use of fabulous animals which might point to a Flemish influence, while the popular use of floral treatment is in a much more English tradition.

These large supports were similar to those on the Elizabethan tables, and were often constructed in the same way, using four pieces of wood glued on to the central core, with the whole unit turned and carved. This reduced the need for using very large pieces of timber.

The shelves or stages were covered with cloth or carpet. In the Turret Chamber at Hardwick in 1601 the court cupboard had a "carpet for it of cloth of Tyssal and black wrought velvet with red and white fringe". When the Turkey carpet wasn't available, a green cloth was frequently used. The 17th century court cupboard had plainer turnings on the baluster columns, which would have shallow carving on the outer faces. The court cupboard was still around in 1696 and Randle Holme mentions that the "court cubbert for viniger, oyle and mustard pot" was among the things "necessary for and belonging to a Dining Room". Although the court cupboard had become unfashionable by the 1680s, it was still made by country craftsmen well into the 18th century.

THE COURT CUPBOARD WITH AUMBRY: 1670—1750

The court cupboard with aumbry has the stage between the top frieze and the next shelf filled in with a canted or splayed cupboard with a door. This later developed into a straight cupboard with doors. These cupboards were usually in three sections and set back sufficiently to allow the two heavy pillars at each end to remain in position. The aumbry was introduced before the end of the 17th century.

One of the problems in the cupboard range is the identity of the livery cupboard. Some writers are of the opinion that the court cupboard with aumbry is one, and certainly a cupboard described at Ingatestone Hall as having a "myddle partician and a bottom" is listed as a livery cupboard. This term *livery* was a "precaution against night starvation" according to one writer, while the *Liber Niger* (1483) explains that every retainer received "for his livery at night,

73

Court cupboard with aumbry c.1585.

half a chet loaf, one quart of wine, one gallon of ale, and for winter livery from All Hallowtide till Easter, one percher wax, one candle wax". The use of *livery* dates back a long way, but the practice died out at the time of the Commonwealth, and was not resumed after the Restoration, although still known in isolated instances into the 18th century.

Another cupboard which has also been considered as a contender for the livery cupboard is a slight variation of the court cupboard with aumbry, being a small cupboard without the heavy frieze at each stage, the recessed aspect of the cupboard is removed and the top columns replaced by corner stiles or with applied split pilasters. The lower potteboard section remains the same, but has slender pillars instead of the more heavily turned balusters which give a much lighter appearance to the cupboard.

It is possible however that the *livery cupboard* is that which R.W. Symonds calls a drinks cupboard, which is shown in the illustrations of contemporary 15th century manuscripts. They could stand in the middle of the room, and were of table height with an aumbry or enclosed cupboard below. The top surface was

Hanging Livery cupboard in carved oak, late 16th century.

retained as a shelf or serving area, and the cupboard below was used for bottles or flagons, while the unit still retained the low pot-boards a few inches from the floor.

The spirit of the livery cupboard is reflected in a couplet of Thomas Tusser (1573),

> *"Some slovens from sleeping, no sooner be up,*
> *but hand is in aumbry, and nose in the cup."*

In time bedrooms were fitted with corner cupboards which took over the duty of holding the night food.

FOOD CUPBOARDS

The food cupboard as such has been clearly defined by most writers as those in which the door or front panels are pierced with fretwork or framed up with turned spindles. These cupboards in early days were called presses or aumbreys, and the piercing of the panel was not only decorative, but obviously intended to give ventilation for the contents. Behind the piercing or spindles would be a backing of cloth to reduce the likelihood of attack by insects or flies. This material was called *haire cloth*. In other cases panels "made of tyn with small

Oak food cupboard, the doors and panels pierced with Gothic style patterns, early 16th century.

holes for aire" were used, and those which were termed a "cawell aumbire" might possibly have been constructed of basketwork.

These food cupboards date from the end of the 15th century and were of several types. They include the standing cupboard or aumbry with legs raising the body of the aumbry off the ground, others were low cupboards likely to be placed on a surface and used as a hutch, while towards the end of the 16th century, narrower food cupboards appeared which could be hung on the walls and these are referred to as *ambries*. They are shown in inventories in the pantry, the buttery and the kitchen, but also appear in the hall and sometimes in the parlour. They may be designated as a *drinke* ambry or as a *mylke* ambry, and there is even a reference to an *ambry pro candelis*, i.e. for candles.

The openwork panel of the 15th century was often replaced in Elizabethan times by the spindles in the door, which were turned in bobbin style up to about 1600 when the baluster style is found. Later the ball turning appeared in the more simplified versions of the Cromwellian period. In the problem of dating, the hinges can often be used as a guide. Early examples of 1470-1550 used a strap or wedge hinge, while between 1560 and 1640 wrought iron hinges of scroll shaped cock's head design, or the wedge and the butterfly type were used. The H-hinge appeared about 1575 but it was not until the mid 17th century that the smaller *butt-hinge* became common, and these were without countersunk screw holes.

The hanging cupboards which were designed for the storage of small items were usually eight inches in depth, and these could therefore be the *'glasse cupboard'* listed in inventories, presumably for storage of drinking glasses. Other larger hanging cupboards were twelve to fifteen inches in depth and are assumed to be drink or food cupboards due to the pierced or spindle framed doors, even though no staining of the timbers appears, which one might expect from cupboards in continual use in this way.

PRESS CUPBOARDS: 1550—1750

The court cupboard, having developed into the livery cupboard and the court cupboard with aumbry, in the 1550s went one stage further and became the *press cupboard*. This type of furniture is also called the *close press cupboard*, the *close cupboard*, and also in later years the *hall* or *parlour cupboard*. In the press cupboard the upper canopied section with its recessed and canted aumbry has a central door and heavy column each side which shows the evolution from the court cupboard, while the lower section, which was earlier than the pot board, is now enclosed, either by a pair of straight fronted panelled doors concealing a single shelf, or by a central door between two fixed panels.

All the panelling in the press cupboard is of framed-up rails using mortice and tenon joints into which the thin panels are free and loose fitting to allow for expansion and contraction. The corner *stiles* extend below the main case a few inches to lift the cupboard off the floor. As with the Livery cupboard the 17th century columns became longer and less ornate, using the vase turning or double baluster outline, and we find by the 1650s that the full column is often replaced by pendant turned knobs or bosses.

About the same time c.1650, the canted cupboard on the upper section gave way to be replaced by a straight cupboard, still recessed with either three sections, or two doors, often using the Cromwellian projecting mitre panels, and the stiles and multons used shallow relief repeating the popular S-scroll design. In early examples the aumbry doors were carved with deeply set arches, and used a variety of acanthus surrounds, floral inlays and even coats of arms. By the 17th century all this was gone, and the carved ornament had given way to glued-on mouldings, and even the bosses and pillars were replaced by split balusters or spindles. These pilasters offered opportunities for secret receptacles, and could be made to slide or lift to create a small *'safe'* for secret or precious items. The recessed upper cupboard section crept forward to present a flat fronted press cupboard of much greater simplicity at the end of the 17th century.

The late Stuart press cupboards were often of a greater length than height, and whereas the normal press cupboard was 5ft 6ins high and 4ft 6ins wide, they could be up to 7ft or 8ft wide. Later examples might also have a row of shallow drawers in the shelf apron, often three in number, and although the press cupboard was no longer used in the more fashionable house after the 1680s, it was still made by village craftsmen into the 18th century. They were generally made of oak in the 16th century, but some in walnut in the 17th century. An Elizabethan revivial in the 19th century made Victorian *'Elizabethan Hall Cupboards'* as they were called, popular in the 1830s and 1840s, but they can be distinguished from the original because they tend to be stained black instead of the more natural nut-brown oak colour, and also they used machine-made 19th century locks and drawers and door knobs.

THE PRESS AND WARDROBES: 1550 onwards

There were press cupboards of different sizes, and the smaller ones were known as *Parlour Cupboards*. It is a useful fact to recall that in medieval times the *cupboard* was used for displaying plate, the *aumbry* as a door fronted cupboard for food and possessions, while the *press* is associated with the storage of clothes. In 1590 Sir Thomas's 'Waynscote press' contained thirty two cloaks, gowns and coats and doublets to the value of £75 10 2d., so we can think of the press in the same way as a wardrobe. It was a cupboard with solid doors, fitted with either shelves for linen and folded clothes or pegs for hanging coats, cloaks etc. Found in the wealthier houses after 1550, it was a variety of aumbry, or to use the medieval French term, an armoire. Nowadays we would call it a wardrobe, but at

Press cupboard c.1610.

the time a wardrobe was a small room fitted for clothes, a kind of dressing room, also called a garderobe. The word wardrobe was also used by Chaucer to describe a privy, so it is the armoire which is the point at which we start its development. In the 14th century it was a simple shelved or un-shelved storage space with doors, for example, (1485) "a grete new standynge almerye with ij levys". Later this developed into the armoire or press with panelled doors, which in 1410 was "a fayere wainscotte presse to hang thereon clothes, with the lock and key". Although usually of plain panelling, in 1600 some were more elaborate, "each chamber hath a press curiously painted and varnished". It was often a high cupboard with sliding drawers or shelves in the upper part, concealed by the panelled doors, the lower part consisting of a row of long drawers. This style persisted in the 1680s, when the press of the richer household would be made of veneered walnut and floral marquetry. The use of tall oak presses allowed clothes to be suspended, but in the late 17th century and into the 18th century the lighter clothes would be folded away on to the sliding drawers which had been introduced.

The large press was 4ft wide and 6ft 9ins high to the top of the cornice. It had two flat panelled doors, five shelves in the upper cupboard part and one long and two short drawers below. The low clothes press was about 4ft by 4ft with a panelled door concealing three shelves, and two further short drawers below the door. This gave the appearance of a tall cupboard set on a chest of drawers. In some cases the depth of the hanging space was increased by making only the lower drawers of the bottom section genuine, and allowing the base of the cupboard to be lower than the front indicated. During the late 17th and 18th centuries much hanging space was still to be found in cupboards set behind the panelling and painted pine wall covering of the bedrooms, but in the middle of the 18th century the major cabinet designers turned their attention to the press and greatly influenced its development.

Chippendale placed the cupboard section of the press on a drawer unit with bombé swelling, using also either bracket feet or canted corner feet. He also used the commode clothes press with serpentine front. The presses of the Adam period had low relief carving with swags, vases on the frieze, and on the door panels contrasting woods and veneers were used.

An important introduction in the middle of the 18th century was the breakfront design with two wings matching the central press section. These wings could be used for hanging clothes, and they were in fact taking over from the clothes press by about 1775-80. However, the more simple pine wardrobe, consisting often only of the central press section, was still made. In the 18th century a convex moulding slip was attached to the locking door to cover the join with the other door, a moulding which became reeded by 1800. Full length doors were introduced on the wing sections in about 1700.

Some wardrobes, such as that of Shearer in 1788, used one wing with pegs for hanging clothes and the other with shelves for linen or folded clothes. The wing door often was full length but with sham drawer fronts on the lower section which matched the drawers on the central section. Hepplewhite speaks of the wardrobe as "an article of considerable consequence" and in his *Guide* uses

Wardrobe of carved mahogany and heavily fielded door panels c.1760, raised on stand with cabriole legs.

satinwood and simple well-proportioned designs with eliptical or rectangular door panels. The wardrobes of the 1820s became hanging wardrobes as we know them today, gradually replacing the press type which lingered on into the Regency period. The plate mirror, which is now an accepted part of the wardrobe, was introduced in 1860.

THE SIDEBOARD: 1750—1837

The use of display furniture for silver, pewter and china, persisted despite the designing of special cabinets for their use, and we find the sideboard and the dresser appearing in the mid-18th century. The sideboard is a term, like the cupboard, of medieval origin, and meant a sidetable. Such tables at first would be table-tops standing on trestles at the side of the hall acting as serving surfaces. Later the loose tops would be fixed to the base section and the framework decorated. In time the side table and the standing hutch (which had a cupboard area) merged to produce the 16th century serving table with panels of gothic tracery in the enclosed cupboard below the *borde*. Before the Restoration the side table had become a small oak table with turned legs and one or two drawers on *runners* inserted into the decorative frieze. By the end of the 17th century the side table was part of the dining room furniture and often took the form of an elaborate piece of walnut furniture, becoming extremely ornate in the Queen Anne and early Georgian Period.

By the 1730s this side table was made in mahogany, and although still basically a table, by the 1750s could have a serpentine form, and after 1740 a marble top or at least one of scagliola (an imitation marble finish).

The move towards the sideboard was signalled with the addition at each end of

Oak side table, early 16th century.

Mahogany sideboard c.1795, with brass rail and curtain.

the side board of a free standing pedestal cupboard topped with urns, usually made of mahogany. Along the back of the table, about twelve inches above the surface, a brass rail was fitted to support the large plate which might be on display. By the 1770s this brass rail sometimes held a short green silk curtain on brass rings, the pedestals were joined to the table forming one unit, and were fitted with a drawer and frieze which continued along the front of the sideboard.

These pedestals had various uses. They might enclose a lead container fitted with taps to act as a wine cooler, or lined with tin and fitted with an oil burner to keep plates warm, and in early examples the cupboard was fitted with two gratings as found in ovens, and below the lower grating was a tripod to hold a piece of red hot iron brought in from the kitchen fire. Otherwise the urns themselves acted as containers for ice or were fitted to hold cutlery. We probably

Regency sideboard with knife boxes, made of rosewood,
inlaid with brass c.1820.

owe the present shape of the late 18th and 19th century sideboards more to
Thomas Shearer than to other designers. Chippendale placed his wine cooler
between the centre front legs of the table, and when the later sideboards used
straight legs in place of the earlier cabriole fittings, Sheerer used the idea of
fitting drawers between the centre and outer legs, with a long drawer across the
centre over the wine cooler shell arch.

These sideboards, with the single shallow drawer flanked by drawers or
cupboards on each side and tapering fluted legs, date from the 1780s. The urns
were removed from the design and replaced with square knife boxes with steep
sloping tops. The drawer-pulls were of moulded and chased brass until the 1770s
when stamped brass backplates were manufactured.

The Regency sideboard continued to be made as a large piece of furniture of

Dresser of carved oak c.1670.

mahogany with brass inlay, and the Victorian sideboards which followed became even larger, and by 1850 had several shelves, capacious cupboards, mirrors, and a riot of carving, usually depicting flowers and fruit. It was in 1710 that the *Tatler* noticed that "the sumptuous sideboard to an ingenuous Eye has often more the Air of an Altar than a table" but it was surely in the Victorian era that this became fact instead of fancy.

THE DRESSER: 1630 onwards

Just as the buffet, the court cupboard and the sideboard were the places for displaying the family plate in the hall or parlour, so the *dresser*, probably evolved from the Norman-French term dressoire, i.e. a side table on which one dressed the food for a meal and from which one served. This has changed from a large, rather magnificent cupboard surface with canopy in medieval times, to a piece of furniture generally associated with the country kitchen or buttery. In the 15th century, the shelves and open hatches in the kitchen were also called dressers, and in *Rites of Durham* (1593) the monks had "their meat served out of the dresser-windows of the great kitchen". In John Earle's *Microcosmographie* (1628) the cook's "best faculty is at the dresser, where he seem to have great skill in the tactics, ranging his dishes in order military and placing with great discretion in the fore-front meats more strong and hardy, and the more cold and cowardly in

85

the rear, as quaking tarts and quivering custards, and such milk-sop dishes which scape many times the fury of the encounter".

When the dresser reappeared in the hall or parlour in the 1630s it no longer had the superstructure, and we are left with a long sidetable up to 7ft long and about 2ft deep. This had a row of drawers below the table top with a number of turned legs along its length supporting the front, while two flat plain corner posts were used at the back. The turning in the front legs from c.1650-1700 were baluster, changing to graduated spiral twist about 1675; we find flat shaped supports about 1670, and the central legs were often missing by the 1680s.

Oak dresser with pewter on display, 17th century, restored.

In some examples there are heavy continuous stretchers about two inches above the floor in the form of a box stretcher. The drawer fronts are *fielded* in Cromwellian examples, or plain panels edged with narrow moulding. Sunk panels were used and these continued up to the 1680s and by the end of the 17th century, flat-faced drawers in the oak dressers were cross-banded with borders or figured walnut.

The table tops of the dressers were finished with mouldings on the front and side edges, and the same moulding was used below the drawers. The dresser without the superstructure was in use during the 16th and 17th centuries, made of wainscot oak, although fruit woods, yew and elm were also used.

The step towards the 18th century dresser took place in the 1690s when a low backboard with a moulded top and sides extended the full length of the dresser top. On the wall behind the dresser a range of shelves was fixed to the wall as a plate rack. They were attached with iron staples and initially had no backing board until the 1720s. The farmer and merchants were reaching for higher living standards, and these shelves would hold a display of ornamental plates and dishes. The early shelves are edged with narrow safety rails at the top and bottom, but in later examples the semi-circular groove appears in which the china rests. The legs of the sideboard were still turned, but in the early 18th century cabriole legs appear.

Several basic types of dressers exist. First comes the *South Wales* or *Glamorgan* type and this is the early Georgian example. It has a dresser top with drawers below, supported by turned or chamfered legs joined at floor level by a continuous stretcher supporting a pot board. Below the row of drawers is a wooden apron shaped in deep curves and pierced with a decoration of hearts or diamonds. Above the dresser top is a plain rack of shelves with a shaped cornice and side supports. A similar design with cabriole legs and straight shelf uprights made after 1725 is sometimes known as the *Suffolk Dresser*.

A second type, which was introduced about 1750 and known as the *North Wales* type has the lower section below the drawers enclosed by doors forming two or three cupboards or two doors with a panel between them. The panels of the doors are generally shaped, sometimes *fielded* and early examples have a half round top to the panel, while later ones have *ogee shaping*. The corner uprights or *stiles* were extended below the cupboard level to raise the dresser off the floor, and the front might have bracket or plainly turned feet. The top of the shelves has a substantial cornice with openwork or a fretted frieze below, and the side uprights might be wavy line sides or turned columns stretching from dresser top to frieze. The North Wales type was also made in Yorkshire and the northern counties, and one type fitted with a clock set in the centre of the plate rack was called the *Yorkshire dresser* and made in the 19th century.

A third type, called the *West Wales dresser* has two cupboards below the row of drawers which flank a kneehole with an arched cove which is known as the *dog kennel*. In most dressers the upper display area is constructed separately from the lower dresser part, but in the *Bridgwater Dresser* the uprights supporting the cornice and drawers come down the side of the dresser to the base. Other varieties include the *Shropshire* and *Lancashire* dressers which have cupboards in the plate racks and are fitted with cabriole legs.

The presence of drawers and cupboards in the display section is quite common, and the spice cupboards as they are called, might be fitted singly in the centre, or one at each side. The *Devon dresser* is one which gives the appearance of a press cupboard, as the display rack is enclosed by doors, so it is only when these are opened that the china comes in to view. The quality of a dresser varied from the plainest cottage example made of oak or fruit woods to the beautiful Queen Anne and Georgian examples veneered in burr walnut, and many exhibit the decorative features of the period. By the 19th century the dressers were, to quote J.C. Loudon in 1839, "fixtures essential to every kitchen, but more especially to that of the cottager, to whom they serve both as dresser and sideboard. They are generally made of deal by joiners, and seldom painted, it being the pride of good housewives, in most parts of England, to keep the boards of which they are composed as white as snow, by frequently scouring them with fine white sand". He had great pleasure in describing contemporary dressers in the Greek and Gothic styles, the former having the dresser section supported by two corner posts turned as Grecian pillars, and in the latter, the display rack was decorated with pointed gothic cut-outs in the side supports, and the cupboards fitted with pointed gothic panelled doors.

THE CWPWRDD DEUDDARN: 1500—1800

A further form of Welsh dresser existed in the 16th century as the *Cwpwrdd Deuddarn* or two-piece cupboard in which the high press cupboard of about 4ft 9ins in wainscot oak or fielded panels, is topped by an upper cupboard with a heavy canopy with pendant knobs or bosses. In the middle of the 17th century a third stage was added to the top as a shelf for the display of plate, pewter or earthware, and this was called the *Cwpwrdd Tridarn* or three piece cupboard. This type of dresser continued in popularity in Wales into the 19th century.

Many other types of cupboard exist for china and other uses, and a regional type of interest is the *haster* which was used to keep dishes of meat or other foods warm in front of the kitchen fire, and in use in the 1780-1820 period. They were designed as an open back cupboard, lined with tin and fitted with a deep middle shelf. It was fitted with castors and when filled with food for the main meal, it could be trundled with the open back facing the fire, absorbing the heat. When the food was wanted, the servants opened the front doors and simply removed it from the shelves. An example of this *haster* survives in Renishaw Hall, Derbyshire.

6 Writing Furniture, Bookcases and Cabinets

The writing desk of the 16th century was constructed to be placed on a table and designed as a box with a slant or sloping front flap hinged at the top. This is probably similar to the desk described in the *Paston Letters* of 1471 as a "wryghtying box of syprese" or that mentioned by Cooper in *Bibliotheca Elistoe* (1584) as a "littell holowe desk lyke a coffer whereypon men do write". These desks could be ornamented on all sides, richly carved or inlaid, or with simple *chip carving* decoration. Their size was about 2ft 6ins to 3ft wide. The writing board hinge had moved to the bottom of the board by the 17th century, so that the flap opened as a writing surface, with the inside of the unit fitted up as a writing interior. The sloping lid left a section at the top of the desk as a narrow flat panel, and this sometimes contained a cavity for pens. After 1650 the writing box was called the bureau, a term connected with the rough woollen cloth used to cover writing surfaces, a material which later became known as baize. In the 17th century tables are listed as covered with *bayes,* which is probably the same material.

By the 1690s the writing bureau was still a separate unit, but began to have a steeper slope and the writing fittings became more elaborate. The bureau boxes were at first made of oak, but after the Restoration walnut came into use, and the bureau was being placed on a special stand rather than a table, which had either solid legs, or gateleg front legs upon which the writing flap could rest. The legs of these stands were bobbin or spiral twist turned, fitting into a flat shaped stretcher a few inches above the floor level, supported on bun feet in the 1720s and on ball feet between 1720-40. The early bureau box with matching stand had a frieze below the box. This frieze was widened and drawers were inserted. After about 1705 cabriole legs terminating in club feet and shaped aprons were introduced and some very elegant small bureaux were produced in the early years of the 18th century.

The stand and legs were replaced by a lower unit formed of a chest of drawers with either straight or shaped front, and by 1695 the bureau box and chest had become one piece and the writing flap was supported by brass elbow jointed stays or small oak bearers called *loafers,* which matched the height of the top false drawer of the chest unit. These loafers had small brass knobs and so could be pulled out easily. The chest usually had a projecting plinth mould. The earlier bun feet were beginning to give way to straight bracket feet. The bureau was made with the same variety of designs, except that the upper section was usually recessed back from the base unit by the slant lid, also defined by Dr Johnson as "a chest of drawers with a writing board". The bun feet which were used up to the 1720s gave way for two decades to the ball foot, but at the same time, c.1710-1715, the straight bracket foot was coming into use. This bracket foot changed during the 18th century with the ogee foot appearing in the 1750s. The woods used were often veneered with burr walnut, yew, elm or olive and usually the carcase or base was deal. The interior of the writing section consisted of parts mainly cut from solid walnut. The veneering of the exterior was often enlivened by inlay in ebonised bands in a crossband, herringbone, or arrow pattern.

The great interest in writing furniture has been linked to the establishment of the postal service and the greater emphasis placed on letter writing.

At this point the precise difference between the bureau and secretaire should be classified. The bureau is a writing box which has a sloping or slant writing flap, and so is any combination such as the bureau bookcase or bureau cabinet. It will then be realised that as the writing flap slopes backwards, the upper section of the piece of furniture is shallower than the base. The secretary or secretaire has a writing compartment which is hidden or covered by either a drop flap, a false drawer or any similar arrangement which is not a slant surface, and tends to be a more upright piece of furniture.

THE SECRETAIRE: 1600 onwards

The word *secretaire* appears early as a *scriptor* in 1679 and as a *scrutoire* in *Bailey's Dictionary* of 1730 where it is described as "a kind of long cabinet with a door or lid opening downwards for the conveniency of writing on". This type of furniture also crops up in the 1710 Dyrham Park inventory as a *skrewtones* which includes other furniture called *writing tables. The fall-front writing cabinet* was introduced into England in the reign of Charles II and formed a development of the cabinet on a stand with two doors at the front which was already popular. With the use of the fall front as a writing surface and the interior designed for writing materials, it had the same function as the bureau, and so the secretary-cabinet was initially made in the same manner. It was supported on a stand with turned legs and a shaped flat stretcher mounted on bun feet. On the Continent the *stand secretary*, without a high cabinet, was superseded in about 1660 by a new form with a central recess for the knees and having two turned legs at the back and four at the front. This appears occasionally in England called the *bureau table*, but it is more likely to be seen in the guise of the gateleg-stand bureau or secretary in which the flap is supported by swinging out from the centre two turned legs which are fitted as gates. As with the slant-front bureau, the secretary was placed on a chest towards the end of the 17th century, and with this development it was possible to create a new writing surface by making the top drawer of the chest a full width false drawer which could be pulled out and the

16th century oak desk with cast iron mounts, fixed to a 17th century oak stand with baluster legs.

draw front hinged down to act as a writing flap. The interior of the drawer was fitted out with the usual pigeon holes and small drawers, as found in the bureau of the same date.

With both the secretary and the bureau, the front of the lower drawers could, as an alternative, be hinged to act as a cupboard, and when the false drawer writing flap was developed the upper fall front was replaced with two doors. A feature of the secretary was the prominent straight cornice at the top of the upper cabinet section with a swelling frieze below called a *pulvenated frieze*. This was matched in the stand and into both friezes drawers were fitted. The secretary or secretaire had many designs in the 18th century, but these still consisted of the upper cupboard, cabinet or bookcase, which was usually flush with the central *escritoire* which Samuel Johnson defines as "a box with all the implements for writing" and the lower set of drawers.

An important finish used on furniture coincided with the importation of Oriental porcelain and lacquer work from the East in the 17th century. John Gay rhymes in his *Town Eclogues*

> "Through ev'ry Indian shop, through all the Change,
> Where the tall jar erects his costly pride.
> With antick shapes in China's Azure dy'd
> There careless lies the rich brocade unrolled
> Here shines a cabinet with burnished gold."

The use of lacquer was particularly popular with richer pieces of furniture and while it was used on a variety of items, there was a continued demand in the mid to late 17th century for Oriental or European lacquered cabinets. The lacquer itself is made from the sap of the lacquer tree and up to thirty different processes of preparation, coating and rubbing down, are necessary when it is applied to a wooden or papier-maché base, before the surface is ready for painting and gilding. Oriental lacquer work includes incised lacquer, where the different layers of colour lacquer, which have an upper black lacquer, are cut through to reveal the pattern in various colours. English lacquer, which was produced by the end of the 17th century, used paint and varnish, and although considered inferior to the harder finish of the black oriental lacquer, was made in a wide range of base colours including blue, red, olive and lapis lazuli. A great deal of lacquered furniture, and panels for insertion in pieces of furniture were imported from China or Japan. In some cases furniture made in Europe (generally in Holland) was shipped to China for lacquering and in due course was returned for sale.

THE CABINET: 1400 onwards

The cabinet, with its elaborate limewood legs adorned with gesso and then gilded, was an admirable match to the lacquer work, and the contemporary oblong cabinets with the elaborate large lock plates joining the two doors, exhibit a high peak in cabinet furniture for ostentation and colour.

The earliest cabinets for storage were much smaller, and in the time of Henry VIII usually contained drawers. They could be used to store papers and valuables. The story is told of Charles I's ring being taken stealthily after his execution to a lady living in Channel Row "on the backside of King Street in Westminster" where it was exchanged for a "little cabinet which was closed with three seals" acting as a secret cache for political papers. When Lady Fanshawe fled from the City of Cork following its capture by Colonel Jeffries, she only hesitated long enough to gather up her husband's cabinet which contained "all his writings and near £1,000 in gold and silver", surely a most useful haul. Other cabinets acted as jewel cases, made of wood covered with contemporary scenes elaborately decorated with stumpwork, a form of embroidery. These jewel cases often had secret drawers, and might be fitted with wooden outer travelling cases, as it was seldom safe to leave valuables at home when travelling around the countryside.

Other cabinets by the 17th century were decorated with lacquer or inlaid with multi-coloured woods, ivory and ebony. In most such large cabinets, the moulded cornice at the top surmounted a barrel frieze which pulled out as a drawer, below which a pair of doors with elaborate locks opened to display an interior consisting of small drawers, arranged around a central cupboard. Below the doors was a matching projecting cornice with another matching barrel frieze inset with drawers supported on a stand made of elm with turned legs linked by a flat stretcher and the familiar bun or ball feet. The cabinets of the 1650s featured pronounced cornices, jutting panels, *string-of-bead* or *bobbin-turned* turnings in the legs and a chest-shaped contour. After about 1680 the turned legs might be replaced by S-scrolled supports.

In the reign of William and Mary there was an increase in demand for the oblong lacquered cabinets which were made without the upper moulded cornice and barrel frieze, and those from about 1690 to 1730 showed fine detail. The cabinet on stand continued in use into the Georgian period, but after 1700 the richly gessoed and gilded stand became more severe in design and in the 1740s onwards they were often similar to the bases of the heavy side tables.

The secretaire, which evolved from the cabinet on a stand had, by the 1740s changed to a writing unit with a secretaire writing unit with a false drawer, known as the *escritoire* below which might be three drawers of graduated depth. The top drawer was a false front behind which the well below the sliding writing surface could be reached for storing private papers or treasures. While the secretary bookcase and secretary-cabinet were still produced, the mahogany secretary tallboy was making an appearance. With this type, the upper section of the secretary was a cabinet with four long drawers designed with or without a decorative pediment. Also designed and popular between 1770-1800 was the breakfront-secretary bookcase with a projecting centre portion containing the escritoire and surmounted by either a broken or scrolled pediment.

The Hepplewhite *secretary* was generally made of either mahogany or satinwood, and was veneered with contrasting woods. There were several varieties of fall-front writing drawers and the later 18th century examples tend to be light in form. The upper cabinet section was usually recessed and fitted with two glazed doors and surmounted by a straight cornice, itself surmounted by a shallow arched or pierced pediment. The late 18th century and Regency period saw more elaborate metal mounts in use. The cabinet-makers of the 1740s renamed the secretaire and bureau the *desk and bookcase* but Sheraton called the secretaire the *secretary* in 1792 and the escritoire or writing section was termed the *inner till*. The bureau and the secretaire developed simultaneously as the cabinetmaker was able to design both with equal ease, and the same element of change in the use of mirrors, glass panes and pediments applied to each. By the time of Adam, the slant-front bureau was no longer fashionable, although Chippendale refuted this idea in his *Director* of 1754 by including several elaborate designs — all with slant fronts. He also inclined towards the use of mirror panels in the doors of bureaux bookcases.

Some early cabinets were designed with two glazed doors and fitted with shelves for porcelain. Samuel Pepys ordered a glazed cabinet in July 1666, and Queen Mary, consort of William III had several made for her collection of Delft and oriental porcelain. These glazed cabinets still had the frieze and cornice and were mounted on a stand. The doors were fitted with small rectangular sections of glass within wooden glazing bars. These continued into the Georgian period where they incorporated the architectural features of the 1730s with the original pediments changing to broken or swan-necked pediments, and the doors flanked with fluted columns or pilasters. These were the china cabinets which were becoming increasingly necessary for displaying the fine porcelain being produced in English potteries in the 18th century.

Technically a cabinet is a case fitted with small drawers or cupboards, and with doors, but this definition was stretched in the 18th century to include these china cabinets with the upper-portion glazed for the display of china. The correct name is of course a China cupboard, and during the 1750s a low piece of display furniture called by that name was in use. It was a rectangular construction of much the same shape as the sideboard, but with shelves, the height of a commode and mounted on short legs. The feature of the china cupboard appears to be the open fretwork — often of Chinese style — behind which the china could be displayed. The use of mahogany in cabinets was common in the mid 18th century, and the china cupboard of the 1750s had in the upper section a moulded cornice and frieze over two glazed doors, with the lower unit consisting of two panelled cupboard doors or two or more bands of drawers.

Cabinet with glazed china cupboard, late 18th century.

The pediments in use were various and applied to cabinets, bureaux, secretaires or bookcases alike. The Queen Anne type was often straight, using cross-grained walnut as a contrast. Another early style was the double hooded or double arch-top, surmounted by two or three finials, with the door frames and the glass following the shape of the pediment. The cornice with the broken pediment terminals of the scrolled swan neck type date from 1720 and contain acanthus whirls which might be gilded. The broken pediment was one which, broken in the centre, had a small space with a pedestal on which a bust or an urn could stand. The swan-neck style was used up to 1800; a pierced pediment has unbacked fretwork included with the pediment. The use of ornamented pediment gave greater apparent height to the furniture at a time when the trend to higher rooms required tall furniture. Other pediments followed the designs of the day, showing Chinese, neo-classic or gothic elements.

The upper doors of the secretaire or bureau cabinet were frequently fitted with mirror glass which in early examples might be cut with a rayed sun or star, and the lower part engraved with figures. The back of the glass was protected by a panel of walnut. In later examples the glass was sunk into the solid door. In the 1680s the bureau-book cabinet was about 42ins wide with two doors, or a single type about 24ins wide with one door. The Vauxhall mirror plate used was produced in quantity by the late 17th century. It had wide flat bevels and was replaced by panelled clear glass by 1740-50.

The introduction of high quality looking-glass into England is attributed to Sir Robert Mansell (1573-1656) who employed Venetian craftsmen to teach the workmen at his glassworks. A form of glass known as Vauxhall Glass came from these glassworks and in 1617 Sir Robert acquired the sole right to make looking-glasses in England. After the Civil War the Duke of Buckingham acquired a patent and re-opened the Vauxhall Glassworks and obtained a similar monopoly, and these Vauxhall glasses were made up to 1780.

The use of clear glass depended on satisfactory glazing bars as sheet glass of sufficient size for cabinet door panels was only obtained with difficulty. Flat glazing bars were the earliest, and after about 1680, heavy half-round *ovolo* bars in cross-banded veneer were used, and then half round bars with an inner fillet in oak up to about 1750. More graceful slender bars cut from Spanish mahogany in the early 18th century allowed the more elaborate designs needed in the Chinoiserie and Gothic cabinets. By 1770 the reeded glazing bar was in use, and the panes of glass themselves were often of geometrical shape, at first octagonal, then in the Chippendale period hexagonal panes were used, with the diamond shape extensively popular from 1800.

In the late 18th century bureau or secretaire bookcase, brass trellis work replaced glazed doors in some cases. Smith, writing in 1808, noted that they were backed with silk curtains which 'gives repose to the eye for nothing can distress the eyes more than the sight of countless number of books occupying one entire space'. The drawers of the early Tudor cabinets had the wide dovetail, but by 1695 the *lap dovetail* was used under veneers, with oak used at first for the drawer lining, and by the 18th century the drawers were made wholly of oak. After 1690 dust boards were fitted between drawers when placed in rows above each other. Where the smaller drawers had concave curving fronts, they were often shaped from solid wood.

The *candlestick slide* or *candle-stand* as it was alternatively called, was a narrow pull-out tray which ran the full depth of the cupboard. This was lined with baize covered brass for fire-safety and so fitted that when the candle was lit, the writing board below was not only illuminated, but also the reflection from the mirror cupboard door added to the light. One candle slide was likely with the narrow bureau, placed just below the doors, with two such slides in the wider bureau. The candle-stand was outmoded by the 1740s when the free-standing candle stand became popular. Both the candle-stand and the *lopers* which supported the writing surface were fitted with small brass pulls and usually made of oak faced with a matching veneer.

PEDESTAL DESK: 1730 onwards

The inventories refer to bureaux and secretaires at the same time as writing tables, but it was not until the reign of George I that the pedestal form of writing table came into general use. It was an open pedestal table with an oblong moulded flat top over a frieze of drawers and supported by a pair of pedestals which contained three or four drawers. This piece of furniture is more commonly called a kneehole desk, and a smaller type of pedestal table was used as a dressing table, particularly by gentlemen, when the kneehole was formed by a recessed cupboard.

By the 1750s Chippendale included several designs for the library or writing table with pedestals in his *Director*. After 1730 they were made of mahogany and the ornamental section *parcel-gilded*. They were designed with carved decoration of Rococo or Chinese style, and supplied with pedestals of *bombé* shape. The kneehole was often flanked by carved pilasters, and the sides of the bombé pedestals canted and embellished with carved or gilt decoration. The Hepplewhite pedestal writing table was mahogany with contrasting veneers and the varieties include straight tops, convex, serpentine and kidney-shaped fronts. The tops were usually inset with green cloth of tooled leather, and the pedestals themselves designed to be either drawer units or cupboards. Sheraton also includes the kidney-shaped pedestal desk in his *Drawing Book*.

THE DAVENPORT: 1770's onwards

By Regency times the pedestal writing table was most popular, and the outer corners were fitted with reeded columns and in keeping with the Regency taste, the use of brass banding and ebony inlay was frequent. A smaller type of pedestal desk appeared in the late 18th century known as a *Davenport*. This was apparently initially made by Gillow for a Captain Davenport, and acts as a piece of military or travelling furniture. However, several repeat orders appeared in the Gillow order books and variations appeared during the early and later Victorian period. It is illustrated in Loudon's Encyclopædia (1833) and consists of a bureau top, usually sloping but occasionally curved, (piano style) mounted over a recessed cupboard into one side of which a series of drawers are fitted. The front of the bureau is supported by two pillars, or pilasters where the cupboard is not recessed, which are set into the protruding arms of a floor stretcher or plinth. The slant lid conceals a fitted writing area, and several slides pull out each side to give more surfaces for books, candles etc. A small gallery surrounds the top of the flat surface behind the slant lid, and in later examples this can also act as a small nest of drawers or pigeon holes.

BONHEUR DE JOUR: 1760—1850

Also of interest is the use by Chippendale of the much lighter and attractive unit which was a writing table and bookcase. A cabinet containing the bookcase or

Early pedestal walnut writing table c.1715.

Two types of Davenport as illustrated in Loudon's Encyclopaedia (1839).

pigeon hole section is set on a small table mounted on tapering legs. This was in many ways similar to the *Bonheur de jour* which was introduced from France c.1760 and consisted of a shallow writing box backed by a small cabinet.

CARLTON HOUSE WRITING TABLE

Of more interest is the Carlton House writing table which was introduced c.1770. Its origin is uncertain, although it was called by this name in 1796. It is basically a writing table on four slender legs with a row of drawers in the apron and a superstructure of drawers and pigeon holes which are fitted around the two sides and back of the flat top writing surface. The upper gallery is generally curved at the corners, giving a D-shape to the table. The writing surface is panelled in leather and the Sheraton design incorporated a central rising easel rest for reading, formed out of part of the desk surface which was made to slide forward. The slender legs were a tapering or *thermed* leg in the 1780s and by 1790 were turned with reeded cappings and finished with ormolu toe-caps and wheel castors. The superstructure varied quite considerably according to the wishes of the client, and the drawer apron could be increased to have a single centre drawer and a band of two drawers each side, the usual length being about 56 inches.

Another variant of the Carlton Table was the *tambour* writing table, in which the same elegant base was used, but the writing top was fitted with a tambour cylinder, opened by sliding back the front curved half of the top. It then reveals a fitted interior with drawers and a writing surface. Hepplewhite noted that it "answered all the uses of the desk and had a much lighter appearance". This sliding lid, the tambour part, consisted of a flexible shutter made of narrow mouldings or laths laid horizontally and glued to a stiff fabric such as canvas, and this then ran between grooved runners to cover the writing surface. This table is illustrated in Shearer's *Cabinet-makers's London Book of prices and Cabinet Work* (1797 ed.) when he suggested replacing the earlier cylinder fall-front with the tambour. This *cylinder fall-front* was the alternative to the tambour, in which the sliding curved portion was not flexible, but consisted of a rounded top which disappeared into the back part of the desk or writing table. At the same time the flat writing surface which was revealed could be pulled forward to give more writing or working space.

BOOKCASES

Prior to the Restoration, the chest was the place for books, as they were scarce, and it wasn't until the 17th century that freestanding or movable bookcases were in use. Shelves for the display of china or pewter were of course made earlier, and hanging shelves, joiner-made of oak, were not unknown in Tudor days. By the time of the Stuarts, rectangular hanging shelves about 30ins high by 40ins wide and 4ins deep are found, with ornamental tops, sometimes surmounted by a cornice or even the two round headed arch. Charles I's inventory of Hampton Court included "nine wooden hanging shelves, gilt £9". Some of these shelves were made for travelling, having wedges to fix them together. Early examples were of oak, but by Stuart times, shelves were often of walnut or of a soft wood gilded. It was not until after about 1690, when the vogue of collecting Oriental china became so widespread that the fixed shelves were preferred. By 1740 the hanging shelves were used where only small quantities were involved. Many such shelves were plain, but the Chinese taste soon made itself felt, and in the 1750s such designs in mahogany were sought after. Chippendale in his *Director* (1754) shows several examples which are "very light but very strong". The fretwork in such shelving was made from San Domingo mahogany which, rich in colour, was hard enough to stand the elaborate pierced patterns used at the time. By the 1770s coarser mahoganies were found suitable for less fine fretwork. This open work was in vogue up to 1800, but solid sides were introduced from the late 1770s with Hepplewhite in his *Guide* (1788) commenting that the shelves "are often wanted as bookshelves in closets or ladies' rooms; they are also adapted to place china on".

The pattern varied, but a standard type had two small drawers at the lower deepest part and the upper shelves were of reducing width. The late 18th century also saw the use of solid backs to the shelves, which made them stronger and more suitable for books.

The use of freestanding bookcases did not come in until the 17th century, and Samuel Pepys was one of the first individuals to acquire standing bookcases, in fact he had twelve such oak bookcases which now form the basis of the Pepys

Library at Magdalen College, Cambridge, being made about 1668. One writer quotes Pepys own words, "reading maketh a full man, conference a ready man, and writing an exact man".

As books became less costly the private collections grew and the widening interest in politics, science and the arts in the 18th century made the libary a most important feature of the country house. However, these tended to be large fitted rooms, and the movable bookcase was still scarce. From the period of Samuel Pepys to the 1730s bookcases were also made with doors and in widths from about 3ft 6ins to 4ft. In time extra wings were added to each side, bringing in the *breakfront* principle found in the bureau, secretaire and wardrobe. The glazing of the shelves' upper section was generally in the form of rectangular panes but after the 1750s more elaborate designs were incorporated. As with other tall furniture, pediments of breakfront, swan neck and pierced work were in use. The lower section was frequently in the form of a cupboard below an ornamental frieze containing drawers, and the whole unit mounted on a plinth.

The *bookcase* was then chiefly an imposing tall piece of furniture with the upper often glazed book-unit raised on a base of drawers or cupboards. The *bookstand* however, made in the 18th century was much lighter, only three to four feet high with open shelves. Usually fairly plain in design, but executed in satinwood or mahogany with the delicate use of brass, and the base of the unit incorporating a drawer set on short feet and casters. These bookstands are also found flanked by pedestal cupboards, and in 1808 Smith raised these pedestals slightly, giving a similar appearance to that found in the sideboard of the period.

Another piece of furniture in which bookshelves are found is a *chiffonier,* where the bookshelves are placed on top of a sideboard type cupboard, and this became fashionable in the 1880s. In his *Household Furniture* (1808), George Smith feels that "in almost every apartment of a house these articles will be found useful. . . their use is chiefly for such books as are in constant use. . . they are also used for china as well as books".

Although the bookcases of the mid Chippendale period were enriched with finely carved details, others were made in a much more restrained manner. Robert Adam relied on faultless proportions, with refined narrow mouldings and he used the breakfront style with a broken triangular pediment. He also employed brass wire trellis in the upper sections in place of glass, backed in many cases with green silk. Some Adam bookcases were painted and decorated with gilt work.

Among the many inventive bookcases of the late 18th century were the revolving bookstands which were either circular or square in section, and in which the shelves revolved around a central pillar fixed to the base unit. The shelves on the circular types diminished in size as the tiers of books rose, and were on a tripod or circular base. The square type was the Victorian answer to the problem of fitting books into circular shelves.

As a development of the display in wainscot or panelling, the corner cupboard was particularly useful, as it encouraged the use of the most awkward part of the room. These cupboards were known from the 17th century, when Charles I's inventory included "one little three cornered cupboard" and they were in general use in the reign of William and Mary for the display of china. They may be divided into three categories: firstly the built-in type which dates from about 1690-1770; the movable double tier type c.1745-1820; and the hanging corner cupboard from 1690-1820.

The built-in cupboard was liked by Celia Fiennes (1661-1741) who wrote that "every corner is improved for cupboards and necessary, and the doors to them made suitable to the wainscot". They were known as *beaufait*, and formed part of the structure, usually consisting of an open unit with an upper section containing curved or shaped shelves, and the lower part either open with a shelf for books, or with a cupboard. By the 1690s panelled doors covering the whole cupboard appeared, then in the Queen Anne period mirror glass replaced the panel, and again by the 1730s to the 1740s mahogany panels or glazed doors were introduced, shaped to fit the upper arch. By the 1750s the glazed china cabinet became fashionable, and the built-in corner cupboard lost favour. These were then superseded by the two tier corner cupboards, as the use of panelling was also replaced by wallpaper or stucco decoration on the walls. They had been in use in the early 18th century, decorated in lacquer, but their popularity increased when made in mahogany. The corner cabinets of the 1740s and later, usually reflected the current style of furniture, for it was important that they fitted unobtrusively into the corner. They were becoming lighter and more elegant in comparison with their built-in predecessors. The two-tiered corner cupboard of the 1750s usually had the ornamental pediment, using such designs as the broken-arch or the swan-neck, and the chamfered sides of the cabinet were often ornamented with pilasters or lattice work. In the later years of the 1790s, the glass panels were once more being replaced by panels of veneered satinwood or marquetry and the cheeks or bevelled sides of the corner cupboard became narrower and the pilasters were discarded. The hinges in use on the cupboard doors were of brass and H-shaped. Except in the country, the standing corner cupboard was out of fashion after about 1820.

The hanging corner cupboards range from about 1690 to 1820, but are seldom mentioned in inventories and were probably kept more for the parlour than the formal rooms of the house. Until the 1760s few were made other than for food and storage of household goods rather than for display. They were probably used in the bedroom in place of the standing livery cupboard and were short and stumpy. By 1700 cupid's bow panels in burr walnut veneer were decorating them, and by 1725 the Vauxhall glass panels were in use, only to be superseded by 1740 by wooden panels and again by clear glazing in the 1750s. After that time some elaborate fret-cut cresting appeared along the cornice, and by Sheraton's period, the hanging cupboard was being made in quantity. This had double doors which were flat and panelled in most cases, with plain moulded tops, the inside was then painted dull green to show off the china.

Later examples of the two-tiered cupboard incorporated a band of drawers or even a full pedestal in the lower section and the ingenious use of desk flaps, fitments or writing tops which could slide out of the unit gave a bureau type writing desk which could be kept well out of the way.

Nursery Furniture

The word nursery conjures up an image of the Victorian nursery in *Peter Pan* with comfortable old furniture and a sharp but devoted nanny in attendance. Children have been provided with their own suitably-sized furniture for many centuries, but this was chiefly limited to the cradle, the chair and the go-cart or baby cage type of arrangement. For centuries the baby slept near the bedstead of the nanny or parent, often in Elizabethan and Stuart days within the shelter and warmth of the bed curtains at night. In some case the truckle beds which slid under the bedstead when not in use, were for the children, and even four-posters were made to children's sizes. Although the Royal babies had their own establishments, English parents were rather backward in placing aside a room for the nurse and baby, and it appears that the original word *'nurserye'* did not come into use until Elizabethan days.

For centuries, the baby was swaddled tightly in protective swaddling bands and in 1495 John of Trevisa recalls that "the nouryce bindeth the chylde togyders wyth cradyl bandes". The cradles were often a simple basket of osiers which was termed a *bassinet*. This had a wickerwork frame and a hood, made of rushes or osiers, and lined with fabric to keep out the draught. The mattress would be quite thick, with a cushion or pillow filled with down, and curtains which could be looped back or dropped to cover the front of the hood completed the infant's bed.

THE CRADLE

Cradles as we think of them are formed by a cot being mounted on rockers or a swing cot slung between two uprights, and the *crib* mounted on legs lifting it high off the ground. It is probable that the early cradle was hollowed out of a log, the natural roundness giving the rocking motion but in fact a *cradle* is usually on rockers while a *cot* swings between two uprights. Possibly the earliest example of the cradle is the oak cradle of the 15th century, reputed to have been made for Henry V. It is interesting to note that a baby prince was usually provided with two cradles, one for actual use, and the other as a piece of State furniture — presumably used at ceremonial and other special occasions. The second was known as the "cradell of Estate". Isabel of France (wife of Edward II) owned both a cradle of gold and one of silver, while a much later cradle, that used by Queen Mary I (b.1516) was covered by a "Yalowe cloth of gold and crymsene

The bassinet, a wickerwork frame and hood lined with fabric.

velvette" and the mattresses were covered with Holland cloth and "filled with wulle". The importance of this state nursery furniture was such that in the 15th century a manuscript (printed in *Leland's Collectanea* of 1552) was written entitled *The christening of a Prince or Princess and the dressing of the Noursery of a Prince or Princess* in which a very full account of the bedding necessary is listed.

I prefer the earlier reference from Piers Plowman (1362) where the author speaks of the mother 'wakynge a nyghtes... to rocke the cradel". While later, John Evelyn writing in the 17th century, confirms that three hundred years later the cradle was still very simple, made of plaited lime twigs. There was a very good reason for the rush cradle. Besides the obvious economy of the cheaper substance, when a child was ill or died of an infection, which was an all too frequent occurrence, then the bassinet or crib could be burned at no great cost, and so not pass the infection on to a later child.

The cradles of the 17th century, the earliest date from which most have survived, were usually panelled in oak with a solid hood, decorated with carving perhaps incorporating some initials or a date. These wooden hoods have been made with small cupboards at the back for the storage of items connected with the infant. In some examples, in place of the carving, inlay in a chequer pattern of holly and boxwood was used. Other woods from which cradles were made were beech, elm, and a variety of fruitwoods. The hoods were also sometimes made to hinge back to allow them to be moved out of the way, so allowing the nurse to pick up the child more easily. The rockers on early cradles were usually inserted into the slit cut into the base of the cradle cornerpost, while in the later 18th century the rockers were screwed into the base of the framework. The body of the cradle was deep, as the baby was sandwiched between a substantial height of mattresses and plenty of covers for warmth. The wooden hood might also be covered with velvet, which was the upholstery often used on Stuart chairs, and it would be fixed in position with gilt-headed nails and decorated with braid and fringes.

The cradles of the 17th century have turned finials, carved panels or chip-carving and the shape of the solid wooden hood could be square or arched or the cradle could be open without any hood at all. The corner finials were useful

Oak cradle with arched hood, turned balusters and finials, with rockers inserted into the cradle framework c.1640.

when the parent or nurse reached out to rock the baby, and could also be used to wind wool on! Some cradles had wooden pins along the inner wall of the cradle, and these were probably to support the webbing where it was used to carry the bedding, or possibly, when higher up the sides, to secure the bed covers.

The nursery was in vogue in the 16th century, and Sir William Ingilby's home had a *nurserye* in 1583, while the Shuttleworth family purchased twelve yards of frieze for the cradle blankets in 1613. This practice of burying the child under a pile of bedclothes was criticised by the diarist Evelyn when his son Richard died in 1658. He writes that his son was "suffocated by ye women and maids that tended him, and covr'd him too hot with blankets as he lay in a cradle near an excessive hot fire in a close room".

THE COT

Stuart cradles were made of softwoods covered in velvet or leather, and the introduction of mahogany in the 1730s did not see an immediate use of this wood in panelled cradles. Instead the mahogany was used for the framework and the panels infilled with wicker with internal cotton or richer materials lining the

18th century swinging cot in mahogany with wire framework for the hood.

Late 18th century cot with swinging mechanism to lull the infant to sleep.

wickerwork for comfort. This change may have been for hygienic reasons, and even the royal babies were accepting such beds. The children of George III were among these, for in 1766 Catherine Naish charged the Royal Account £13 2s. 5d. "for a superfine split wicker cradle very large, a pair of neat mahogany rockers to do with carved roses". These cradles were the cot type slung on turned mahogany posts supported by a link-stretcher at floor level. Catherine Naish supplied several such cradles, and in 1766 she also supplied for Prince William (later to be William IV) "a neat mahogany couch bedstead on casters with mahog. laths and pillars, two neat frames the whole length of the couch with turned Bannisters to keep the Prince from falling out". This then was the crib type which is so popular in the 20th century, but probably with fixed sides rather than the vertical sliding side we are accustomed to. The laths referred to in the bill would be the horizontal laths which act as an open floor to the crib on which the mattresses rest.

Later swinging cots varied in elaborate designs, even going so far as to have tent canopies, but they remained basically the same construction. Sheraton, however, utilised a swinging mechanism devised by Mr Holinshade of Drury Lane which he "contrived to lull infants to sleep with". This used a clock spring, and when started would automatically rock the cot for at least 20 minutes, although a period of an hour and a half was aimed at. By the end of the 18th century, the wood and wicker, or cane swing cots, were being made in quantity, in a fairly uniform pattern, and they appear to have largely superseded the low rocking cradles.

HIGH CHAIRS

After the child has outgrown the cradle, cot or crib, he is very soon sat very firmly into his high chair where he can be fed with comfort, and also take his place at the dining table without being over-awed by the height of the table. An early reference to a child's chair is listed among the effects of Robert Sidney, Earl of Leicester, for in the wardrobe at Leicester House in 1558 was "a little chair for a childe, of carnation and greene clothe and tinsell" although we don't know if it was high or low.

The high chairs were usually made in the fashion of the chairs in vogue at the time, the only concession being the wide splay of the long legs for stability, the smaller seat, and the two holes in the arms to take the restraining bar which stopped the child from tumbling to the floor. A child could be set in the high chair from the age of four months, and examples of high chairs date back to the 17th century. An early high chair, c.1620, is of the chair on table type, where, instead of long legs, the chair, which is of oak finely inlaid in Holly and Boxwood, is in the wainscot style and it rests on the base of a turned stool with the back legs rising to form the thick backstands of the child's chair.

Child's oak chair c.1620, inlaid with holly and bogwood.

Walnut and cane Restoration high chair c.1680.

Others had the solid approach of the Commonwealth backstool, while following the Restoration of Charles II, we find fine examples in walnut of the turned and caned Restoration armchair with cane seat and back panel. This chair is missing the footrest, but the front legs have in the centre of each of the three turned bobbins, a hole on each side of the chair in which the footrest would have been fitted, with the other two holes allowing for the child's growth.

The 18th century saw the child's high chair firmly influenced by the designs of Chippendale which are shown in the Chinese carved frieze on the heavy outward curved legs and the attractive line of the top cresting bar. The child, when a little older, would be given a low chair, and these show much more clearly whether the craftsman could marry the diminutive size desirable with the strength of structure required in nursery furniture. No such niceties were observed in the joined child's chair in the Victoria and Albert Museum which is inscribed with the date 1687. Here the heavy splayed back panel is echoed by the rake of the front arm supports and stumpy legs — but they produce a very solid and much abused piece of furniture. The turner's child's chair was also a favourite, and a

Child's oak armchair c.1687 with turned arm supports.

Astley-Cooper's Corrective chair of painted wood, early 19th century, designed to encourage children to sit up straight at table.

17th century miniature *carver* chair with rushed seat met most of the needs of the young child. A century later the Windsor chair makers, working in yew and elm, were producing early examples of children's Windsor's for which many styles were created to meet the demand of the 19th century.

A favourite type of child's chair was the wing rocking chair, which also had a pot-hole in the seat. These wing chairs were made of oak, walnut, and pine, and the pots were made of pewter or wood. Actual rockers were not added here, as they formed part of the side supports of the chair.

THE BABY CAGE

When the child could sit up and take notice, the baby-cage, baby-trotter or go-cart, which taught him how to walk, came into action. This consisted of a framework which supported the child, but left his arms free, having small wheels or casters it could roll across the floor in the direction the child wished to go. These were known in the Middle Ages, and appear in paintings of the 17th century. They are made of wood in two basic types. Firstly the circular or square framework which has a ring supporting the child, and secondly a square box-like frame in which the child walks, pushing the go-cart along.

The earliest type consisted of a square wooden frame on casters, which were probably originally broad leather or wooden rollers, above which a square table-like surface was linked by four sloping legs to the base frame. In the table top was a round hole into which the infant was lowered, but his arms were kept above the hole to stop the child from falling through. Later, by the early 17th century, the flat top was sometimes replaced by a circular ring, often covered with upholstered velvet, which was half-hinged to open and allow the child into the baby cage. Several of these cages were made with elaborately turned sections, and small wooden wheels which could swivel within the wooden joints which held them in any direction. The go-cart became very popular in the 18th century, and in *Nollekens and his Times* (1828) we are told that these go-carts were very common in every toy shop in London and in greatest number in the far-famed turners' shops in Spinning Wheel Alley, Moorfields.

The second type was more of a go-cart, i.e., a small square framework with turned balusters, having small wooden wheels in the base of the four corner posts. The child went inside the frame, hanging on to the top front rail, and so staggered along pushing the go-cart in front of him.

There are examples of small chests of drawers and even small tables, varying from gateleg to refectory types, but in general these were not necessary, as the highchair ensured that children could sit at normal table height, while the chest of drawers, being used chiefly by adults, did not have to be of a smaller size.

Not all children's furniture was intended to be comfortable. The eminent anatomist and surgeon, Sir Astley Paston Cooper, President of the College of Surgeons, brought out in about 1800, his corrective chair which gained much favour. It was a very high chair with a straight back and legs which flared outwards to give the necessary stability. Its purpose was to train children to sit upright. Loudon, writing in 1839, adds that it was recommended with the view to prevent "children from acquiring a habit of leaning forward, or stooping; the upright position of the back affording support when the child is placed at table, and eating, which a sloping backed chair does not". He adds, in all fairness, "It is proper to observe that some medical men do not approve of these chairs".

Another piece of furniture was created out of the high chair, called *jump-ups*. These consisted of a small elbow chair fitted to a stand, stool or table to which it was fastened by a thumbscrew. When the chair was unscrewed it revealed a table at which the child could sit when the days of the high chair were over. Such a table was approved by Loudon who adds "the table is made lower than a chair, in order that the nurse may have the more power over the child when she is washing it".

112

Chairs and Seating Furniture

Although in ancient times seating furniture was known, the use of chairs in England was almost always restricted to persons of rank. This was done possibly to enable the user to appear to dominate his immediate circle, but also for him to be seen more clearly by the rest of his followers. So a platform at the end of the hall and a high architecturally designed chair promoted the right image. The joined chair which has survived from these times was the product of the joiner and owes much of its design and method of construction to the Gothic churches being created at the time. These chairs echoed the European movement of the early Middle Ages, when craftsmen moved from country to country, and kings sought out the artists and architects from abroad to build and design new wonders.

THE JOINED CHAIR: 10th—16th Centuries

This joined chair was therefore the principal Gothic prototype chair and it was made from the 10th century well into the 16th century. The design might well have evolved from the chest, which was used in early times as a chair, and in some instances the seat of the joined chair lifts to disclose a chest for clothes or books, creating the alternative name of *close chair* for this heavy piece of furniture. The feature of the joined chair was the linking together of the heavy timber uprights with mortise joints pegged with wooden dowels, and the infilling of the structure with wood panels or boards, hence another name of *post and boarded*. The vertical supports for the framework were called *stiles* and the horizontal members known as *rails,* and these held the panels firmly between them, reducing the need for very wide planks. The arm-supports and the areas between the legs were filled in with wooden panels, matching the back, and making a solid looking chair.

Although heavy, the problem of their mobility comes into question. Randle Holme in his *Academy of Armoury* (ms.1649) comments that they were "so weighty that it cannot be moved from place to place, but still abideth in its own station, having a kind of box or cubbert in the seate of it". Yet the 1466 Ewelme Inventory shows that the Duke of Suffolk travelled with "a chaire of tymbre of astate covered wt blue cloth of gold and panells of copper". This chair had also a "case of lether thereto" into which it could be placed when taken to pieces for travel.

Joined oak armchair, late 16th century.

The famous Coronation Chair in Westminster Abbey is one of the few very early joined chairs to have survived. It was made for Edward I by Walter of Durham in 1299, and when the *Stone of Scone*, upon which the Scottish Kings were crowned, was brought to England it was incorporated in the seat. The style is typical of other chairs which are illustrated in the manuscripts and paintings of the medieval period.

THE X-CHAIR AND FOLDING CHAIR: Medieval to Stuart Period

As well as the joined chair, two other types were currently made, these were the *X-seat* and the *thrown* or turned chair. The ancient X-chair exists in examples from Pompeii, but by the Middle Ages, Pauline Eames considers this chair to have become an "expression of supreme majesty". It was used by Philippe I as early as 1082 and up to the coronation of Pope Boniface IX in 1389 as a form of throne. The folding nature of the X-chair made it ideal for use in soldiering, and was also associated with ecclesiastic furniture. The inventories of St Paul's Cathedral (c.1241) show us that there were five iron chairs of which one was given by G. de Lucy, Dean of St Paul's who died in 1241, and another described as "a Bishop's seat of silvered iron, with gilded human heads". The X-chairs of the Tudor period were quite elaborate, having a series of x-supports stretching across the depth of the seat and the seat itself, the arms and back were upholstered and covered in rich fabric, finished with silk fringes and velvet cushions. In some cases the whole framework itself was covered with fabric.

THE GLASTONBURY CHAIR: 16th—18th Centuries

The later wooden folding chair known as the *Glastonbury chair* was introduced in the 16th century and made of planks joined together with wooden pins. The curved back, which was slanted backwards, extended down to the surface of the wooden seat and the arms, which were hinged by a wooden bar, were shaped to support the elbows. The notable decoration is carved in the back in very stylised flower effects enclosed within a lozenge, often headed or topped by the sunflower motif. These chairs are believed to be based on the chair belonging to the last Abbot of Glastonbury who was executed in 1539. It is illustrated in Henry Shaw's *Specimens of Ancient Furniture* (1836) and on the top was carved *Monachus Glastone* and on the arms *Johanes Arturus*.

THE WAINSCOT CHAIR 16th—18th Centuries

Following from the earlier joined chair was the *panelled chair* more commonly called the *wainscot chair*. With this the whole outline becomes lighter and less architectural in nature. It still retains some of the heavier elements of the original construction, and presents some of the formality of the old chairs of state. Particularly noticeable is the difference in the turnings of the legs and arm supports, which are slimmed down and the open arms, which have a downward sweep from the back. The seat becomes narrower, and the backs, which were often in the past simply panelled, now have attractive inlays formed from box, holly, pear, bog oak and sycamore. The motifs of floral sprays, which often spring from a vase surrounded by small birds were the favourite, while the use of chequer patterns was common.

The backs had a top rail surmounted by a cresting of elaborate carving, and the uprights or *backstands* as they are called, were topped with carved finials. The legs were joined by continuous floor stretchers, and the front legs and arm posts were often fluted. The later examples show the cresting becoming higher, and involve additional scrollwork, while the legs are linked by side stretchers in place of the floor stretcher. By 1650, they had a spirally-turned stretcher higher up joining the front legs. These wainscot chairs were made from the 16th to the early 18th century in country areas and some of the Elizabethan periods became still lighter in construction, the seat narrower and the back panel slimmer until a type of chair known as the *caquetoire* appeared.

THE CAQUETOIRE: 16th—17th Centuries

This chair was probably of French origin, and was found in England from the time of Elizabeth through to about 1625. An English example in the possession of the Society of Antiquities of London, is dated 1585. The tall narrow back with its bold carving was in the Renaissance manner, and the carving often took the shape of a lozenge which encloses a head surrounded by carved foliage. These chairs were often made of walnut, and an identification feature is the widely splayed arms and legs giving a very triangular effect to its appearance. The actual name *caquetoire* means to chatter, and it is sometimes called a conversation chair, designed, as one writer adds "primarily for women"!

THE BACKSTOOL: 17th—18th Centuries

Another development of the wainscot chair came from a variety designed with an open arcade back. The 17th century saw this develop into the Derbyshire and Yorkshire backstool or side chair.

As mentioned previously, the use of chairs was limited to a certain upper class of persons, and the number available even in a royal household would be limited. At Hengrave, an inventory of 1603 notes that the Great Chamber had 32 joined stools and only four chairs, while at The Vyne in 1541, out of fifty two rooms, the inventory listed only 19 chairs. The social aspect is emphasised in the story by the herald who accompanied Princess Margaret who was the daughter of Henry VII, on her journey to meet James IV in 1503. Apparently when James came to supper before their wedding, he "satt in the Chayre, and the Qwene abouffe him, on his ryght haund, For, because the Stole of the Qwene was not for hyr Ease, he gaffe hyr the sd Chayre". So it is obvious that only one chair was available, and normally even the Princess would not have sat up on it.

So the stool was, with the bench and settle, the more normal seating furniture. In most cases this stool was a joined stool, for in the hall or dining room they would be made to match the table and other fittings. The joined stool, like the joined chair, was made of a framework of thick oak rails and heavy turned legs which were joined and secured by pegs or dowels. This was topped by a seat of thick planking. At some point in time, probably between 1600-1640, these stools were developed so that the back legs continued up beyond the level of the seat forming *backstands* between which, above seat level, a framed or solid wooden back could be fitted, thus creating the *backstool* which was our first *side* or *single chair*. Such a stool would be similar to that mentioned in the Shirley inventory of 1620 from Faringdon in Oxfordshire, which refers to "a stoole with a back; two chayres and one back chaier", thus seeming to include three stages of the development in one sentence.

It will be appreciated that in order to preserve the true dignity of the armchair owner, these new chairs were not treated as proper chairs for some time, and in fact, backstools were made up to at least 1760. The creation of this backstool, and the development of the arcaded version of the wainscot chair produced a combination at the time of the Commonwealth, just before the Restoration, which is known as the *Derbyshire* or the *Yorkshire* chair according to its form of design. The *Derbyshire* chair has an arcaded top rail linked to a central rail with turned balusters or spindles, and is ornamented with knobbed finials. The front legs were turned, the back legs plain, and a continuous floor stretcher was used, plus two higher stretchers linking the side legs. The *Yorkshire* chair was very similar in design, except that the back was infilled with usually two or sometimes three broad flat rails or cross pieces which were hooped and escalloped, decorated with drop pendants and carved with stylised designs. In some instance the pattern incorporates a head with a pointed beard, believed to commemorate the execution of Charles I and then to be known as mortuary chairs.

THE CROMWELLIAN CHAIR: 1640—1700

During the Commonwealth period (1649-60) a lack of decoration and ostentation is the aspect which comes first to mind, and the Cromwellian chair with its leather upholstered plain seat and back echoed this theme. It was an angular oak armchair or side chair, for both were made, of a somewhat uncomfortable shape, with turned armposts, knobbed legs and front stretcher. The side stretchers were usually plain with one each side at floor level and another higher up. The solid back panel, raised at least twelve inches above the seat level, was, like the square seat, covered in leather, occasionally lightly tooled and fastened to the frame by rows of brass headed nails. The arms were also upholstered in leather with the sides picked out in brass studs.

THE RESTORATION: 1660

With the death of Cromwell in 1658 and the later collapse of the Protectorate, Charles II was invited to the throne and returned in 1660, a date known simply

Derbyshire back stool, late 17th century.   Oak Yorkshire backstool, late 17th century.

as *The Restoration*. He didn't come alone, and England saw the introduction of crafts and furnishing materials which had been denied to the population during the Commonwealth period. The Royalists who were returning from a period of exile, brought a new approach to comfort in furniture, and the use of walnut and cane began to replace the earlier hard oaken seats.

THE CAROLEAN TURNED WALNUT CHAIR: 1660—1700

One of the early chairs of the Charles II period was the spiral turned walnut chair of about 1660 which probably acted as a forerunner to the finer chairs of the 1680s. It was called an *arming chair* a term introduced around this time to mean an armchair, made in a square shape of spiral turned framework. It had a floor level H-stretcher and two higher front and back stretchers, and the back panel, which started at arm support level, was constructed of four or five vertical spiral turnings in an oblong framework. The seat, made of wood, was dished to take a cushion. This chair would appear to be the last in a line of turned chairs which in the later 17th century evolved into the Windsor chair.

118

Carolean turned walnut chair, caned seat and back c.1660.

Triangular oak thrown or turned chair, early 17th century.

THE TURNED OR THROWN CHAIR: 15th—18th Centuries

This was one of the basic types, made, unlike the joined chair or X-chair, by the turner or village wheelwright. Their origins, it is suggested, go back to Byzantine furniture, and they are shown in manuscripts of the 13th-14th centuries. By the end of Elizabeth's reign, they were made in the form of a triangular armchair, with a triangular wooden seat and a low back from which the arms sloped downwards to the arm supports. This back leg, at the apex of the triangle, extended upwards and was heavily turned, and a large number of decorative spindles were fitted into the sides and base of the chair with almost geometric precision. The joints which linked the framework were dowelled, sometimes pegged, and they were made in an entirely different technique from the contemporary joined chairs which were mortised and tenoned.

Whilst the chairs were frequently triangular, there are exceptions, and a very fine example is in the Welsh Folk Museum, which illustrates this technique in a four legged thrown chair. The dating must in certain locations overlap into the late 17th century, as they were very decorative and a much sought after design.

119

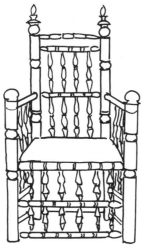

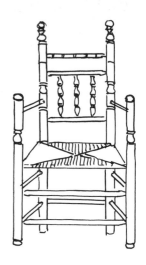

The Brewster Chair c.1660-1700 named after William Brewster, one of the original Pilgrim Fathers.

The Carver Chair, c.1660-1700, named after John Carver, first Governor of the Plymouth Colony.

Some smaller examples also survive, but the really fine thrown chairs tend to be in museums and country houses. Littlecote Manor, near Hungerford, still exhibits the travelling chair of Sir John Popham (d.1607) Chief Justice of the King's Bench, who used it at assises, and which due to its continual use and moving from place to place, shows signs of wear at the feet.

In their simpler form, and in a style which appears in the United States of America, the turned chair is linked to the names of John Carver and William Brewster. By the mid 17th century, life in the colonies had become established, and the standard of living had risen to the extent that some luxury and comfort crept into the timber homes which were being built to replace the earlier homesteads. The earliest types of chairs to emerge as an identifiable native style are those which bear the names of two prominent New England leaders.

The *Carver armchair*, which is linked to John Carver (1575-1621) is dated c.1660-1700, and usually made of maple, ash or hickory with rush seats. The turned front legs rise above the seat to form the arm supports and the back legs extend to become the frame posts for the back. Two turned horizontal rails in the back are linked by three or more vertical spindles and this unit is surmounted by another turned vase-and-ring rail. The back posts have *steeple-turned* finials, and one or two arm rails join the back uprights and front arm supports, a simple box stretcher is used for the underframe. This was probably a style which existed in England and was popular enough to be used as a pattern by the travellers as they settled in the Colonies.

The *Brewster armchair*, named after William Brewster (1567-1644) was more

120

elaborate than the Carver, although built on the same lines. The main difference lies in the considerable increase in the amount of turned bobbin work. The single row of spindles in the Carver is replaced with two rows, the lower one has the spindles extending into the back rail. The front stretchers are turned and two rows of spindles extend along the front of the seat, almost touching the ground. Beneath each arm, extending down below the seat level on each side are further rows of spindles.

THE RESTORATION WALNUT AND CANE CHAIR: 1670—1700

It is a great step forward from the turned chair of the 17th century and the backstool of the 1640s to the Restoration walnut and cane chair of the 1670s. This new type of chair probably originated in France, spread to Holland and then to England. Frequently the turnings will indicate the country of origin. It is a tall chair, somewhat rectangular in shape, noted for its fine turning, carving and pierced work. This is very apparent on the wide front stretcher and cresting rail, and a very new feature was the use of cane panels in the seat and back, sometimes called *five crowns* chairs.

The wood used was a rich brown French walnut, with dark veinings which, when carved, lightly oiled and waxed, had a fine texture. The English walnut was a lighter coloured wood, and as the grain was coarser, tended to produce a less crisp finish in the carving. Cheaper versions of the Restoration walnut and cane chairs were made of beech, stained to resemble walnut.

The uprights in the back of the chair, the legs, armposts and the side and back stretchers were spirally turned (barley sugar style). The flat front stretcher, often four to five inches in depth, was carved shallowly with Restoration motifs, which often incorporated cherubs and crowns, known in the inventories as the "boyes and crownes" or, with rosettes, thistles, female heads, vines etc. This stretcher was designed to harmonise with the flat cresting rail at the top of the chair which was cut in full relief, and flanked on each side by the turned and carved finials of the tall backstands.

At first the arms were flat, but from about the late 1670s they were curved in section, and instead of being straight they dipped in the centre and were scrolled over the arm supports in a cyma curve. The arm supports or pillars varied from baluster turnings to very flamboyant vertical S-scrolls. The seats were framed to take the cane and so were tenoned into the sides of the back stands and front legs. The outer edges might be round moulded, and in almost all examples would be carved. With later single chairs from about 1685, the front legs were often let into holes bored into the underside of the seat rails.

The use of cane followed the Restoration and according to a petition of the 1680s "about 1664 cane-chairs came into use in England, which gave so much satisfaction to all the Nobility, Gentry and Commonality of this kingdom (for their durableness, lightness and cleanliness from dust, worms and moths) that they came to be used in England and sent to all parts of the world". By the 1670s caning had become a specialised craft, and the cane which was used was brought from the Malay Peninsular. After the knots and rough surfaces were removed from the natural rattan, the cane was split into quarters and the pith removed. It was then split into very narrow strips. The caning up to about 1670 tended to be coarse with an open mesh, but a finer weaving with a still narrower cane came in later and the various patterns of caning developed.

The spindle turning in early cane chairs developed into the *swash turning*, a climbing barley sugar twist, which by 1675 was used freely. The turnings were interrupted by square sections at points where the mortise and tenon joints linked parts of the structure. After 1670, the *baluster* turning, which had been so popular in the late 16th century, was revived and often replaces the spiral turning with advantage. The twist turning itself had national characteristics. The English turning tends to have a narrow rope with deep hollows; the Dutch turning is a rope which is thick and the twist close and rapid. The leg turnings generally terminated in bun feet, but with elaborate chairs anything from scrolls to carved animals' feet and hoofs may be encountered.

The back panel was usually enclosed within the cresting rail and a lower rail about four to six inches above the seat. On the sides it was often flanked by upright splats which matched the front stretcher, and the cresting rail had carved and pierced decoration. Towards the end of the 17th century, two panels or a variety of pierced splats often replaced the single panel. Variations included an oval panel, although these have been considered to be more characteristic of French or Dutch chairs.

By the mid 1680s the chair became lighter in construction and the carved and pierced splats and stretchers appear more delicate. By 1690 the back took up a slant-back appearance. Obviously some attempts to add extra comfort were made, as in 1680 a chair sold to the Queen was described as "a caned chair with elbows to move with joynts and a footstool with iron workes to fold". For the King, an entry in the Lord Chamberlain's Accounts tells us that a cabinet maker made models of walnut chairs "to show the king".

THE FARTHINGALE CHAIR: 1580-1700

The Cromwellian chair with its plain leather covered seat and back panel, made some attempt at comfort and similar to this style was the *Farthingale* or *Turkey-work chair*. An upholstered side chair brought in during the late 17th century with a floor level continuous stretcher was probably constructed to meet the problem of the enormous hooped dresses of the period. Originally the farthingale was a Spanish style and the whalebone hoop was a hazard when a lady attempted to sit down. To use an arming chair would be to court disaster, but the wide upholstered backstool with its low back allowed the great hoop to rest more gracefully with the dress draperies flowing to the ground.

They brought in fashions strange and new,
With golden garments bright,
The farthingale, and mighty ruffles,
With gownes of rare delight.

These chairs were made during the whole of the 17th century, but in the 1660s the diarist Evelyn writes of the arrival of Charles II's Queen "with a train of Portuguese ladies in their monstrous farthingales..." indicating that the style was already out of fashion in England. The design of the chair closely resembled the back stool and much of the woodwork was covered with damask, matching the padded seat and back, or the knotted pile turkey-work wool on a canvas base was popular, resembling the pile on turkey carpets. The legs and stretcher were often plain, but the front legs were also found in a plain column shape. This chair was also called an *imbrauderer's chair* or more commonly an *upholsterer's chair* and John Gloag notes that they could be bought by the dozen or hired from the upholsterers when the occasion arose.

THE RESTORATION WING CHAIR: 1680—1720

The upholsterer did not lose out completely when the cane chair was introduced into England in the 1660s, for in about 1680 a tall, well upholstered wing armchair came to England from the Continent, and in contemporary inventories it is called an *easie armchair*. It had straight deep wings which were designed to shield the user from draughts, and the square raked back panel dropped to within a couple of inches from the upholstered seat. The arms were straight and well padded, being supported by either barley-twist turned pillars or scroll supports. The legs and stretcher, like those of the Restoration walnut and cane chairs were, according to their dating, turned in spiral or baluster turnings or scroll curves, and the front stretcher heavily carved and fretted. In one type of this wing chair, the wings were fitted to the frame with a ratchet device which let down to make it into a sleeping chair. By the 1700s the back panel had dropped to the level of the seat, and the wings were now an integral part of the framework, and were shaped in an S-bend curving into the turned-over arm which was also filled in. The upholstery was taken down to cover the seat frame, leaving only the legs and stretcher showing. By about 1700 the cabriole leg was in use with these chairs.

RESTORATION UPHOLSTERED WALNUT ARMCHAIR: 1680-1730

Of the same period is the walnut and gilt armchair with a high rectangular back, raked backwards from the seat. The seat itself and the square back panel which does not reach the seat level, are heavily upholstered, the seat finished with a

123

deep fringe. The open arms, are both outward scrolled, cyma curved and resting on scrolled armposts. The legs and stretchers are heavily carved in the baroque manner and the front stretcher, like its other Restoration counterparts, is wide, flat and symbolically carved and pierced.

WILLIAM AND MARY PERIOD: 1680—1702

The Continental influence in design is still noticeable in the Dutch lines seen in the furniture of the William and Mary period, and this was supported by the number of Dutch cabinetmakers who followed William to England after his accession to the Throne. An important aspect was the way in which the earlier rather straight lines of the chair, gave way to curved lines in about 1700. Still using walnut, the framework became lighter in weight and design, while the height of the chair became very tall, making them the tallest chairs to be made in England with the possible exception of the 20th century MacIntosh chair. This increase in height, linked with the lighter construction, made them somewhat weaker in strength. The backstands were undulating and the shape of the splat and the curve fitted into the small of the back, making them very comfortable. This shape is called *spoon-backed* due to its similarity to the side view of the curve of a spoon.

By 1700 the uprights were often turned over into a shoulder, with the disappearance of the finials, from which the hooped cresting rail sprang, and this rail, together with the splat, was carved and pierced, with the splat made slimmer and shaped resembling a vase, the lower rail connected to the seat framing. These chairs with their turned uprights and the high crest carving rolling into scrolls and foliage gave rise to the name *periwig chairs* because of the resemblance to the curls of the wigs worn at that time.

The turned legs of the earlier period continued up to the 1690s, but they were often turned with mushroom or pear-shaped capping below which the leg tapered to a ring rest on a serpentine X-stretcher with a raised finial, below which in turn a small bun foot gave a sturdy effect. About 1700 the cabriole (or bandy) leg came into style, this followed the line of the long shallow S-curve used on the later Restoration chairs, and the leg terminated with a pad foot or cloven hoof foot. Stretchers were still used. The chair seats could be either caned or upholstered. Some later chairs bore the influence of Daniel Marot, a Huguenot who was driven from France in 1685. In his position as architect to William III his influence was considerable, and his designs are recognisable by their elaborate detail.

QUEEN ANNE PERIOD: 1702-1714

Although it was not immediately apparent, the chair backs were beginning to come lower, and the striving for comfort appears in the shape of the back. The

Restoration walnut and cane armchair c.1680.

Carved walnut chair with early cabriole leg in the style of Daniel Marot, early 18th century.

feature of this popular style was a simplicity of decoration, sound construction and rather elegant lines. The ornamental splat was replaced by a simple vase design and this apparently plain chair was known as the *bended back* chair or more commonly as the *fiddleback chair*. The reason for the term *fiddleback* was the waisting in of the backstands resembling the shape of a violin. The legs were simple cabrioles and the result was a tidy dining chair which has been made ever since. In the 19th century the armchair version was called the *Hogarth chair* due to its use in a self-portrait by that artist, and the names have since been somewhat interchangeable. Soon after 1710 the claw and ball foot was adopted as the terminal of the cabriole leg, although the pad or club foot was still used well into the 1750s. Seats were now being upholstered on removable frameworks. The cabriole leg, which at first was narrow and slender, began to bulge at the knee, and from 1710-25, the *broken* type was common. The shield appeared, carved on the knee, and by 1730, the pony-foot termination was in vogue.

With the finer chairs the splats, backstands and seat rails were veneered in burr walnut, and although the cabriole leg was used at the front of the chair, it was seldom used for the back. The stretchers remained in use into the 1710s, but were not found so frequently from 1715 onwards.

GEORGIAN CHAIRS 1714-1730

The period leading up to 1720 saw the fiddleback walnut chair change from its lightness of construction and lack of ornament to a much more solid and stronger looking chair, square in form. It now had heavy cabriole legs, with knees crisply carved with shells, scallops and shields, and the legs terminated in carved lion's paws, claw and ball feet. This square effect was obtained by widening the seat and lowering the height of the back. The splat, which had earlier been vase-shaped and slender in form, became more eccentric in design, and wider, often with shaped sections reaching horizontally to the sides of the backstands, thus filling up much more of the back of the chair. The cabriole leg is normally fixed to the base of the seat rail — but in the 1720-1730 period several examples show it *hipped* to rise above the level of the seat rail, becoming more an integral part of the design.

With the armchairs, the arms are set back from the front of the seat, no longer an extension of the front legs, and the arm pillars rise from the side rail of the seat. The arms were generally curved to fit the elbow and scrolled over the arm pillar for comfort.

With the duty taken off imported mahogany by the Act of 1721, this wood came into use in chairmaking in the mid 1720s. As it was hard and close grained, it carved with a crisp finish. However, the early chairs showed little change in design to the walnut predecessors they were replacing. Between 1720-1735 there was a feeling towards decoration in chairs once more, and the use of the lion mask is typical of the period.

WILLIAM KENT INFLUENCE: 1727-1740

This use of decoration led into the baroque style with the use of architectural elements in the design introduced by William Kent. He was among the architects who incorporated the interior decoration, the furniture and furnishing, into his brief when designing a building. Kent made great use of gilt and parcel-gilt, as furniture with this finish showed up well against his more restrained Palladian interiors. One criticism levelled against them is that they were somewhat heavy in design; Horace Walpole called them "immeasurably ponderous". One architectural change introduced by William Kent was the Library and Salon in place of the earlier Long Gallery, and this created an opportunity for new forms of library furniture and among these the *library chair* and the *reading chair* were introduced.

THE WRITING CHAIR: 1720-1770

The writing chair which was introduced early in the 18th century is found in two types. The early one, c.1720-30, was an arm or elbow chair in which the arms were set back to allow the user to sit with the chair drawn up to a desk or table. This is also called a *compass-seated chair* or a *spoon-back chair*. It had the spoon back shape and in some of them the dip in the centre of the cresting was to allow the queue of the user's wig to rest out of the way. The front legs were heavy cabrioles with ball and claw foot. The design was noted in 1736 as it allowed the dress-conscious gentleman to sit when "the plaits of the coat stuck out very much in imitation of the ladies' hoop", acting in a similar manner for men to that of the farthingale for women.

The other type of *writing chair* was also known as the *corner chair* or the *Queen Anne library chair* from which it evolved. Again the heavy over-carved cabriole legs are used, but four this time, spaced with one at the centre front, one centre back and one each side. The seat was shaped to a serpentine or diamond shape, and the back had a half-round crest rail at arm height above the seat supported by pillars interspaced with pierced splats. The arms had a bold outward scroll and the back rail had the crest scrolled over. This chair was in use from c.1730 to the 1770s, and later examples had an extension at the back in the centre of the cresting which rose to head height giving it the name, *barber's chair.*

THE READING CHAIR: 1720-1820

The reading chair was also called a *conversation chair,* a *cockfighting chair* or a *horseman's chair.* It was made of walnut or mahogany and upholstered in leather, on which the user sat facing the back of the chair, resting his arms on the wide flaring horse-shoe shaped crest rail. The seat itself was pear-shaped, wide at the front narrowing to about ten inches at the back where the narrow back supported the crest rail. This usually incorporated a reading desk and often candlestick rests. By sitting this way, the rather splendid coats of the gentlemen would not get creased. These chairs were introduced about 1720 and remained in use to the 1820s. A famous example is the chair in the Victoria and Albert Museum believed to have belonged to John Gay. This has a drawer in the seat with a secret compartment behind, while out of the widely flared arms slide brass hinged trays. In 1757 William Canty advertised in the *London Gazette* that he was able to supply from his shop at St Mary-le-Strand "mahogany and walnut-tree reading chairs, corner chairs, compass-seated chairs, shaving chairs and dressing chairs", which shows the wide variety of chairs available at this time. Sheraton includes a reading chair in his *Cabinet Dictionary* (1830) "to make the exercise easy and for the convenience of taking down a note or quotation from any subject".

THE FRENCH PERIOD: 1735-1750

In the *London Magazine* of November 1738 a writer comments on the "ridiculous imitation of the French taste (which) has now become the Epidemical distemper of this Kingdom!" This was the *rococo* (rocaille) style derived from France which originally was used to describe the grottos and gardens at Versailles, and was fashionable by 1740. Although it might be considered somewhat similar to baroque, it was actually a reaction against the flamboyance of the early 18th century decoration. Rococo exhibits a more restrained use of scrolls, cartouches and gilt work, being particularly applicable to the upholstered chair.

THOMAS CHIPPENDALE AND 'THE DIRECTOR'

It was the French rococo which Chippendale modified to the English taste and described as *modern style* in *'The Director'* pattern book which he published in 1754. Up to that time the cabinetmakers in England had to evolve their own designs for the most part, copying where possible and modifying where necessary. When Chippendale published his designs in 1754 he presented the three styles of furniture in vogue at that time. First came the *modern style* based on the rococo of the 1740s; then came the *Chinese* or *Chinoiseries style* which evolved following the publication in 1741 of *Travel in the Chinese Empire'* by du Halde; lastly came the *Gothic* style in which the contemporary fashion, led by Horace Walpole, in re-creating the period of the Stuarts led to a style believed to be a revival of Jacobean furniture, but which, in fact, lifted certain aspects of design from several centuries and merged them into this *Gothic Taste.*

Thomas Chippendale (1718-1779) was born the son of a village carpenter at Otley in Yorkshire, and it appears that he was sent up to London and apprenticed there. He set up business with partners, and at the age of thirty six, published *The Director* which was probably the most ambitious venture of its kind to that date. He was also a highly successful businessman and the furniture with which he is associated is of the highest craftsmanship.

In his rococo chair, Chippendale used the open back with a pierced splat in its vase form, but with elaborate strapwork interlacing ornament. In the use of mahogany, the hardwood allowed delicate designs, one of the more popular being the *ribband-back*. Seat frames were square and of the *slip type,* or the seat rail was covered with the seat fabric. The crest rail he used was a cupid bow serpentine shape with the ends turned up in one type, or turned down in another to curve into the backstands. The legs were cabriole with claw and ball feet, but in about 1750 the square slightly tapered legs with box stretchers were used.

For the Chinoiserie motif, the open back was infilled with a delicate pagoda-like fretwork, and the same motif was incorporated in the brackets of the seat rail. The cresting bar might have a pagoda shaped outline and the square legs

Reading chair in carved mahogany c.1725.

were carved with *card-cut* lattice-work. The Gothic chair with its open back still had elements of rococo into which were grafted a pierced window splat of gothic tracery, with gothic *card-cut* lattice work in the legs and seat-rail.

The design of the country ladderback came into Chippendale's hands, and he produced a mahogany ladderback which was popular c.1750-90, having flared backstands and the three serpentine cross-stays pierced and carved with the crest rail in a similar serpentine shape.

ROBERT ADAM AND NEO-CLASSICAL DESIGN

Around 1760-65, chair design began to show the influence of Robert Adam, and following the discovery of Pompeii, Adam's use of classical design was much sought after. The designs became lighter, the cabriole leg was abandoned for the straight tapering leg, and he designed a crest rail as square backed, hooped or serpentine, then ventured on to oval, heart-shaped and even shield-shaped backs.

GEORGE HEPPLEWHITE DESIGNS: 1770-1790

The chair backs designed by Hepplewhite were simple and graceful, and while he may not have been the originator, his distinctive shield back chair is the one with which he is associated. He also employed the heart-shape, oval, circular and square back, and his upholstered chairs used the French influenced *cartouche* shape. In this design the chair backs did not always meet the seat, but were supported on extensions of the legs rather than regular backstands, which made for greater freedom of shape. His splats incorporated several motifs, including drapery festoons, wheat-ears, urns, medallions, and the Prince of Wales Feather. He was also fond of the *banister back* in which three or more upright banisters were incorporated in the shield back, and he used circular backs with radiating designs.

The legs favoured by Hepplewhite were generally straight, square and tapered, sometimes with a spade foot or similar terminal and fluting or reeding was the decoration he used. The dipped seat was introduced in about 1760 and was used by Hepplewhite and Manwaring. His ideas were incorporated in *The Cabinet Maker's and Upholsterer's Guide* which was published by his wife in 1788, a short while after his death. In it he trys to "unite elegance and utility, blend the useful with the agreeable", but he does not pretend to be original, claiming that he only wishes to "follow the prevailing fashion, omitting such articles as were the production of whim". Peter Darby sums up his work when he says that Hepplewhite "developed the Neo-Classical style of Robert Adam into a more domestic style suitable for everyday use".

Regency chair in beech, japanned black and gilded, with sabre legs, c.1810.

The richness of the baroque of William Kent gave way to the rococo of Chippendale and to the classicism of Adam, and in the last years of the 18th century Sheraton was able to add elegance and refinement. He abandoned the curved emphasis which Hepplewhite had placed on much of his work, and instead favoured the straight line, which is apparent in many of his designs. There is a fragile delicacy in Hepplewhite which becomes even more noticeable in Sheraton's early work. Some of his work was japanned and he re-introduced the use of cane in the seats and back panels of his chairs. As with Hepplewhite his chair legs taper, are slender and more often cylindrical. The back panels often terminate four to eight inches above the seat. Sheraton used mahogany and also softer woods such as beech, painted to match the hangings of the rooms for which they were designed. The decorations on the chairs include flowers and garlands, highlighted with gold.

In Sheraton's late work the French Directoire style influenced him. The top rail became broader and was scrolled over, and the infill of the open chairbacks sometimes included latticed panels. His later designs are incorporated in *The Cabinet Directory* (1803), and some of the elements of the following Regency style can be seen there.

REGENCY PERIOD: 1800-1830

Many of the features of the late Sheraton styles lingered on into the Regency, in particular the emphasis on the horizontal, and the use of the *sabre leg* which sweeps forward while the back legs sweep back. The square backs retained their low profile but the arms of the open armchair tend to sweep down from a high point on the back uprights.

However the geatest influences of the Regency period were the archaeological contacts with Egypt, Greece and Rome. The designs were taken freely from the ancient sources, and were frequently added to standard designs to enhance the simpler forms of the late 18th century chairs. Thomas Hope (1770-1831) published his *Household Furniture and Interior Decoration* (1807) in which designs adapted from the past were transformed into furniture for the stylish home, while George Smith, in *A collection of Designs for Household Furniture and Decoration* (1808) felt he was offering the best examples of the Egyptian, Greek and Rome styles, together with some taken from the Gothic or Old English fashion, or 'according to the costume of China'. So we find lion's paws and leg terminals, supports in the form of sphinx and lotus leaf. In certain instances Smith replaced the formal carving by brass as appliqué or solid cast finials and motifs.

The return of the Chinese taste which had been in vogue in the mid 18th century was possibly due to the interest shown in the style by the Prince of

Wales, and this was brought to its most extravagant peak in the work done for the Brighton Pavilion. For the less rich there was japanned furniture and beech chairs painted to look like bamboo. After the Regency era the period of the individual craftsman was largely over, as the machine determined many of the designs, and the necessity for greater volume of production reduced the variety of individual detail. The 1830s was also the period which saw the mass production of the Windsor chair, one of several country chairs which had evolved in a sequence parallel to others of finer craftsmanship.

THE COUNTRY CHAIR

Following the Restoration period, the backstool completed its metamorphosis from the stool to the side chair, going on to be treated by the designers of the 18th century in many different ways. In the 17th century however, early types gradually divided into three or four main styles which emerged as country chairs, evolving from the *Yorkshire, Derby* or *Turned* chair. The *Yorkshire* chair was the sturdy oak chair with two or three arched and cusped horizontal rails. This was the forerunner of the ladderback chair. The true ladderback was revived as a rushback chair in the 17th century and was still known in England in the 18th century as a *Dutch chair*. Over the years the horizontal splats show many varieties and in the early 18th century, the cupid's bow outline can be seen on chairs with a simplified cabriole leg. As the chair designers looked around for new ideas, the ladderback was adopted and became respectable, and in a serpentine shape was adapted in mahogany using pierced slats. In 1760-1770 there were even more elaborate ladderbacks in the drawingrooms with pierced geometrical shapes which show the influence of the Gothic Revival. The country style ladderback was very simply made, having any number of horizontal slats, from four to seven, and in some more elaborate examples a fan-back effect involved the use of slats of decreasing width. The slats themselves might have the cupid's bow outline, the double ogee shape, the straight bottom and curved upper line, or an elaborate ribbon shaping. As the ladderback was of traditional cabinet style chair construction, the legs were shaped rather than turned, and a type of rural cabriole leg is to be found in the 18th century chairs which is particularly attractive.

The North of England appears to have been heavily involved in the production of ladderback rush and wooden seated chairs, and although there are many variations in design, they fall into two main categories. Firstly, those with the ladderback slats open at the top, and secondly those where a cresting bar links the backstands above the upper ladder slat. In the first group, the *wavy line ladderback* (which is among the earlier ones, similar to a Hogarth print of 1730) and others which bear the same basic details, are called *North Country Ladderbacks*. The second group tends to be called *Wigan Ladderbacks* as they are thought to have originated in that town. There are probably greater differences in this group than in the North Country chairs, with chairs from another area which are known as *Macclesfield chairs* bearing sufficient resemblance to be included in the same category. In the Victorian period a shortened version of the ladderback was used extensively as a church chair, and several million must have been made in High Wycombe alone for that purpose, as in the case of large churches and cathedrals as many as four thousand were ordered at one time, which were chiefly of the *Wigan* type.

The *Derbyshire chair* with its two cross rails and linking spindles or balusters was probably the forerunner of the *spindle-back chair* which is associated with Lancashire and the North of England. It was also made in Yorkshire and Cheshire but it appears that the main concentration of chairmakers was in Lancashire, and certain designs can be linked to specific towns. With the common design, the side chair had two rows of spindles in the back of the chair, separated by a cross rail, and the lower rail raised about six inches above seat level. The armchair or *carver* was higher and often had a third row of spindles. The chair usually had a bobbin turned front stretcher and variations depended on the type of ornament used for the crest rail. These include the *nipple-top,* the *sunburst* (which has a shell ornament or sunburst carving in the upper centre position) while the use of the serpentine shape crest rail into which the backstands merge, produced the *Chippendale spindleback.*

Perhaps more elegant than the normal spindle chair is the *Dales spindle-back* which is believed to have originated in the Dales of Westmorland, Cumberland and North Yorkshire. This is of a much lighter construction and incorporates only one row of spindles, longer than normal, below which a slender cross stay infills the gap left by the absence of the second row of spindles. This is the pattern which probably influenced William Morris when he created his *Suffolk Chair* in the later 19th century.

Although the ladderback and the spindleback chairs dominated the North Country scene, the Midlands was the centre for the *Windsor Chair* which evolved from the 16th century turned chair, and appeared in the late 17th century as the turner's and wheelwright's chair. Unlike most country chairs, it had very early in its life also been made in fine woods and for the wealthier clientele. In 1724 the Duke of Chandos had seven japanned Windsor chairs made for his Library at Cannons, and the *Accounts of the Royal Household* for 1729-33 record that Henry Williams, *joiner,* supplied a very neat mahogany Windsor chair for the Prince of Wales Library at St James for the sum of £4, which was quite a considerable amount in those days.

The early chairs were *comb back Windsors* which had a flat crest-rail which might be shaped in Chippendale style, cabriole legs and an ornamental splat. In the 1760s the Gothic influence, which was then popular, dictated the design of the wonderful *pointed arch Gothic* with wide *window splats,* and the bow-back,

134

Goldsmith comb-back Windsor chair mid-18th century.

Wheelback Windsor chair c.1820.

with splats of different designs were in use quite early in the 18th century. The well-loved *wheel-back* Windsor is believed to have been introduced in the 1770s while the familiar *Prince of Wales Feathers* splat is a reminder of the Windsor's popularity in the Regency period. Although these Windsor chairs were made in various parts of the country, the largest concentration of chairmakers producing them was in the Chilterns and Thames Valley area. Here the cottage craft of the late 18th century grew into a major industry, until in the 1870s over 4,700 chairs were being produced a day in High Wycombe.

STOOLS

From the Medieval and Tudor days there have been three basic type of stools. firstly the *trestle type* in which the seat is supported by two *truss-ends* or *standards* linked by a double underframe, which were keyed with a plank top. This trestle type was made from the 15th century at first in oak and then in walnut. The second type was the *joined stool* which had a board seat and was supported by a

135

framework consisting of a square continuous stretcher at floor level, linked to a square seat rail resting on four turned legs. The whole was mortised and tenoned together, and the joined stool was widely made into the 18th century. The third type was the plain *turned stool* with the seat supported by three of four plain or turned legs socketed into the underside of the seat. This was also called *stick furniture.*

Of these the turned stool is probably the oldest, and is also called a *fotyd stolys* (i.e. the footed stool) but they were not always too safe, as the legs had no support, an aspect brought out in *The Castle of Perseverance* (c.1325) when the world is likened to "a III foted stole, it faylyt a man at his most nede". In the 15th century the trestle stool existed, with their splayed uprights shaped in many ways and the link-underframe pierced or carved with Gothic motifs. In due course the trestle stool was framed up to become the development of the joined stool. The decoration of these stools usually existed in the frieze, (which might have chip-carving) in a shaped underframing, and in the turnings of the legs. These turnings usually followed the pattern of the tables and chairs of each period. Initially in the 16th century they had slender columns with fluted swellings. This gave way in the 17th century to the heavier bobbin, ring and ball, and simplified versions of the cup and cover designs. The stretchers were very low, often at ground level, but by the mid 1600s were well off the floor. These joined stools were provided with cushions, but the 1590s saw them padded and upholstered, although the board seat joined stool continued into the late 17th century. These upholstered stools could be made in sets and in matching material to that of the chairs or drapings. The Earl of Northampton's inventory of 1614 included "eight high stools of tawney velvet with cases". The use of velvet with fringes was common, and they would be embroidered or interwoven with metal thread which would still glisten after the basic material had worn or faded. Another popular covering was a knotted pile called *turkey work* which was reminiscent of the pile of a Turkish carpet. The use of the term *high stool* probably indicates a stool which is contemporary with the Farthingale chair and which met the same need. They were made with the painted woodwork and the seat padded, upholstered and finished with a fringe.

Following the Restoration and the introduction of the walnut and cane chair of c.1580 comes the walnut stool of similar appearance, having scroll legs, an elaborately carved wide flat front stretcher and a turned H-stretcher linking the round legs. Going into the William and Mary period, the base of the stool changes to straight legs and scrolled feet with a serpentine X-stretcher in the 1696-1700 period. The double stool came into vogue, stretching from four feet to seven feet in length, and by 1710 the cabriole leg becomes prominent. It ranged from a simple plain type with club feet to the more richly carved cabriole with acanthus leaves on the knees and with claw or claw and ball feet.

The influence of Chippendale's Gothic taste becomes apparent in stools of the

18th century cabriole leg stool.

1760s when fretted legs, card-cut seat-rails and latticed suports change the whole character of the stool. This goes much further with the *window stool*, designed as a double stool to set in a window alcove. Here the two ends are brought up to fifteen to eighteen inches above the seat and scrolled boldly over, carrying the seat upholstery over with the curve.

SETTLES AND BENCHES

Where stools were not used to sit at the table, the bench and the settle were to be found, and the benches were generally trestles, which in the early 16th century were the solid *truss-end* type with the underframing tenoned through each truss-end, and the protruding ends pegged in position. By the 17th century these solid ends were often replaced by splay turned legs linked by a continuous floor stretcher making the bench more in keeping with the construction of the joined stool.

The settles were at first generally built into the fabric of the walls, or, if movable, were very solid and massive. They had panelled backs which could vary from waist to head height, and the arms and sides were panelled to match the seat, which often took the form of a panelled chest with a hinged lid. Such settles can be identified with that described in the inventory of Henry Field (1592) as "a wainscote bench", and as Shakespeare in Henry IV (1695) talks of "sleeping upon benches after noon" they can be seen to accommodate several people.

By the 1650s the settles were of lighter construction, the arms open, and the lower chest section replaced by a seat rail, turned legs and a continuous floor stretcher. Only the panelled back and the presence of arms distinguishes the settle from the bench. In 1655 the settle went one step further when, with the design of the Cromwellian chair in mind, we find the oak *settle* or *settee* with

Chippendale style ribbon-back double settee.

open arms, leather upholstered seat, and back open to the height of the arms above which the leather upholstered back panel rises to neck height. The turnings are bobbin, and the leather studded with brass headed studs — showing the link with the actual *settee*.

Although the settee was introduced early in the 17th century, few were made until after the Restoration, when in many cases chairs were extended and modified to make room for two or more persons. This could be done by combining two or three chairbacks, lengthening the seat and inserting extra front legs to carry the weight. Another method was to produce the *daybed* which consisted of a long walnut stool-like structure, caned, richly carved in the Restoration manner and fitted with a hinged and adjustable back-rest at one end and usually an array of fitted cushions. By 1685 this day-bed had the back-rest fixed permanently in a slant position and the whole reclining surface upholstered. During the early 18th century the legs and carving changed to match that of the chair furniture and by the mid 1700s the day-bed had been forsaken for the greater comfort of the more generously upholstered settees and sofas.

The settee evolved from the settle, and so can be considered a new type of furniture. It was upholstered and covered with rich fabrics, finished with braid and fine fringe trimmings. In the William and Mary Period, some are found with the very high back associated with the chairs of that time, and also the upholstered walnut chair with wings is modified to act as a settee with the arms upholstered and scrolled over, and the seat set on low turned walnut legs and elaborate serpentine X-stretchers with finials.

The Queen Anne settee moved forward to use the cabriole leg and dispensed with the stretcher, while the back height was considerably reduced. A more significant change in the settee came about in 1720 when the *double* and *triple chair settees* made in walnut and then in mahogany, came into vogue. The open-back arm chair with upholstered or drop-in seat was made up in lengths of two or three chairs, and the styles religiously followed the chair styles as they were made up as parts of a set. Here can be seen the beautiful Chippendale Chinoiserie and Gothic designs made to match the side chairs, and only in a few cases has the cabinetmaker found it necessary to adapt the design to flow across the whole back, instead of meticulously reproducing the double or triple chair design.

In the early 18th century the upholstered settee progressed, following the baroque architectural style of William Kent in the 1720s, and then with gilt legs and seat rails, open or upholstered arms, they also illustrate the rococo designs of the early Chippendale chairs. About the 1750s the sofa, as distinct from the settee, came into popularity. The difference lies in the use rather than in the design, as the settee was made for several persons to sit on, so tended to be upright and of normal seat height, while the sofa on the other hand is for reclining or resting on. It would often have the Grecian couch shape with a roll-over arm or roll cushions at each end. As with the settees, they had gilt or carved mahogany frames with rich upholstery.

By the 1770s the much lighter construction came into use in the settee, and the slender elements of the shield-back and the round-back chairs found their way into the much more delicate settees with the use of cane appearing in the Hepplewhite style seat and back panels. Perhaps the most noticeable change is found in the rather extravagant designs of the Regency Period, when boat-shape settees, sofas carved with lions and many other bizarre motifs came into use.

Another type of settee, called the *hall settee*, usually made of wood alone and not upholstered, found its way into the large entrance halls and galleries of the 18th century. While it is true that these hall settees still follow the designs of the chairs, they are of a more austere pattern, and surely reflect the slower rate of change to be found in parts of the fashionable house which were less used by society.

Cabinetmakers, their Designs and their Trade

It was not unusual for the main 18th century cabinetmakers to work from a good address — a place where their noble clientele could visit without losing face. Seddon's of Aldersgate had "a very large commodious brick building, the façade adorned by a row of nine columns" which was known as London House, while William Linnell undertook his business in a large double-fronted house at No 28 Berkeley Square, where they "had a select and fashionable clientele and their charges seem to have been similarly egregious".

As early as the time of Samuel Pepys, it was the practice for the client to visit the establishment of the craftsman. In October 1668 Pepys "set out by coach to the Upholsterer's in Long Lane, Alderman Reave's, and then on to Alderman Crow's to see a variety of hangings and were mightily pleased therewith, and spent the whole afternoon thereupon; and at last I think we shall pitch upon the best suit of Apostles where three pieces for my room come to almost £80". These were tapestries, and another time Pepys persuaded Mr Harman, the upholsterer "to take measure of Mr Wren's bed at St. James's, I being resolved to have just such another made me".

Another famous person, the actor David Garrick employed Chippendale to furnish his new house in the Adelphi. He ran up a bill of nearly a thousand pounds, and after paying off on account more than a third of this sum, neglected to make a final settlement with the firm until threatened with an action-at-law. In another instance the cabinetmaker John Lennell did much work for William Drake of Shardeloes in Buckinghamshire. On receiving the bill, Drake submitted it to another cabinetmaker for his opinion as to whether he was overcharged, and indeed in the opinion of the cabinetmakers, Linnell had overcharged by 20%. Thomas Chippendale moved into the select area in Midsummer 1752 when he leased Somerset Court in the Strand. This was recorded in 1720 as a "handsome new-built court with houses fit for good inhabitants", and he leased it at a rent of £27 per annum. The block had a ground area about twenty feet wide and forty-five feet long, backing on the south wall of Northumberland House. While at Somerset Court it is probable that Chippendale became known to the Duke of Northumberland, as it is to this noble that his major design book *The Director* is dedicated. The business seems to have grown, for in 1753 he moved to St Martin's Lane, the 'Harley Street' of the furniture trade, where other prominent cabinetmakers such as William Vile, James Cobb and William Hallett were in

141

business. During 1754 Chippendale built workshops, warehouses, a timber store and shop, and equally important, continued publication of his design books.

The 18th century saw the printing of several books of furniture designs which in the earlier years had only formed part of the pattern books produced by architects and artists as part of their work in promoting the building of modern houses. The *City and Country Builder's and Workman's Treasury of Designs* (1740) by Batty and Thomas Langley emphasised the baroque style of William Kent, while in *A New Book of Ornament* by Matthias Lock and Henry Copland the rococo elements became noticeable. The eccentric designs of the mid 18th century were brought into focus through the use of Chinese taste in the pattern books of others such as *New Book of Chinese Designs* (1754) by Matthias Darly and the *Rural Architecture in the Chinese Taste* (1750-55) of William and John Halfpenny.

Perhaps the high point of English furniture design came with the publication of Chippendale's *Director* of 1754, as, for the first time, the book was devoted entirely to the designs of furniture, and was also the first to be published by a practising cabinetmaker. In it the three main *tastes* of the time, the Rococo, Chinese and Gothic were catered for. This design book was soon followed by others, including Ince and Mayhews *Universal Systems of Household Furniture* (1759-63); Hepplewhite's *Guide* (1788); Thomas Shearer's *Designs for Household Furniture* (1788) and Thomas Sheraton's *Drawing Book* (1791-4).

It should not be assumed that these were all original designs, or even the work of the named designer. One writer notes "although Chippendale's signature appeared on the plates, it seems that he cannot claim sole credit for all the designs". In the same way, the claims made that this or that piece of furniture was by Chippendale, or Sheraton, are difficult to substantiate, for the design books provided the means for a competent cabinetmaker to construct identical furniture. So the terms *Country Chippendale, Irish Chippendale* or *American Chippendale* can fall into place and not confuse the situation.

It would have been a matter of importance to customers and cabinetmakers alike when an advertisement such as that which follows appeared in *The Boston Evening Post* of January 5th 1767.

> *Cox and Berry arrived from London...*
> *beg leave to acquaint the public that they*
> *have...*
> *the following very useful books viz —*
> *The Cabinet and Chair-maker's Real Friend*
> *and Companion, containing upwards of 100*
> *new and beautiful Designs of all sorts of*
> *chairs. Crunden's Joiner and Cabinet-maker,*
> *Carvers etc.*

For here was the opportunity of re-furnishing in the latest fashion and maintaining the *English* look which was so much a part of the Boston social life.

In England, the customer, as mentioned before, would buy direct from the workshop, and by 1700 the shops were notably growing in size, displaying a greater range of goods. In 1713 Daniel Defoe writes about the "increase in Retailers of Trade" as being among the evils of the day. He comments that if the reader would "view the famous churchyard of St. Paul's, what takes up a whole row there and supplied the place of eighteen or nineteen topping drapers — cane chair-makers, Guilders of leather, Looking-Glass Shops and Pedlars of Toy-Shops". In fact in *A General Description of All Trades* (1747) the cabinet shops are described as "so richly set out that they look more like palaces, but his business seems to consist as do many others, of two branches, the Maker and the Vendor".

To make themselves known, the craftsman would have a tradecard or handbill. These were printed for handing out to customers and to passers-by, and added to the name and location of the furniture maker would be details of his line of work:-

> *Henry Newton, Upholsterer, At the Three Tents,*
> *the corner of Cullum Street in Line Street,*
> *near Leaden-Hall Market, London.*
> *Maketh up & Selleth all sorts of*
> *Upholsterers Goods,*
> *Chairs, Cabinet-work & Glasses, with all sorts*
> *of Teeks, Feathers, Quilts, Blankets, Coverlids*
> *& Ruggs. Household Goods Bought and Sold &*
> *Appraised. Likewise Funerals Performed.*

These cards frequently were engraved with examples of the furniture sold, and so act as a useful guide to the speciality of each craftsman.

To identify his furniture, and let others know who made it, a maker's label or stamp might be found on English cabinet work. While this was obligatory in France, the practice was not commonplace in England. However, there were two types of label found on furniture. One was an actual trade-card or handbill such as that used to publicise the maker, the other a smaller, proper label. The latter was usually circular and usually only gave the name and address of the craftsman. They often appear to have been cut by a pair of scissors from a larger sheet in which they were printed in rows.

Although cabinetmakers seem to have introduced the use of trade-cards and labels about the time of the Restoration, joiners seldom used them, tending to brand their furniture with their initials, a practice dating from the 16th century, if not earlier. The reason for marking furniture was of course not only a means of identifying the maker, but also a means of 'preventing abuses'. This was a term which the toolmaker Thomas Cranford used when in 1703 he advertised that he

143

William Russell's handbill c.1770.

"maketh and selleth all sort of Joyners and Carpenters Tooles, where any Artificers or Merchants may be furnished with greater or lesser quantities of the best sort, and to prevent abuses I mark with my Name at length instead of T.C.". By the end of the 18th century the stamping of the maker's name in full on the carcase of the furniture was being used instead of labels. Gillow of Lancaster in particular adopted the practice. The shops or workshops themselves adopted a sign which could be used on the trade card and also displayed on or over the premises in which they worked. The emblems or signs most popular among the cabinetmakers fall into several groups. They include, of course, those which symbolised the specialised part of the trade which they practised such as *The Chair, The Bed, The Looking Glass, The Three Tents* (sign of the Upholders' Company) or *The Three Compasses* (which appears on the arms of the Joiners' and Carpenters' Companies). Other signs were patriotic such as *The King' Arms* or the *Crown and Sceptre* — in fact many signs show much more a resemblance to the traditional inn signs than what we would consider as trade signs, with the *Spread Eagle* the *Half Moon* or the *Three Nuns* sounding very much out of character.

Small Ad. selling was as prevalent in the 18th century as it is today. In the *Daily Post* of February 16th 1731 was the following full advertisement.

To be sold by hand
This Day and To-morrow (the lowest price being fix'd
on each Particular, without any abatement)
At SURMAN'S Great House in Soho-Square, St.Anne's
all the entire Household Goods. . . Likewise all the
fine works of the noted Mr James Falcon,
cabinet-maker and Glass-grinder: The Goods consisting
of Standing Beds and Bedding, Large Glass Sconces in
carv'd and Gilt Frames, fine Wallnut-tree Desks and
Book-cases with Glass Doors. . . .

So the list continues for several inches of column space. The interesting point is that this self-same advertisement appeared 119 times between February 16th 1731 and September 26th 1732, as well as in other papers including the *Daily Journal.* So it is obvious that there was a constant supply of Mr Falcon's furniture, and that in the same way as we still see a great amount of *Ex WD goods* in immaculate condition today, someone was cashing in on Mr Falcon's reputation and making them to order.

The Mr Surman whose name appears in the advertisement, acted for other cabinetmakers and dealers, and in one advertisement which commenced to run in October 1732, he is selling the goods of a Mr Thomas Tennant "an emminent Wholesale Dealer in all manner of Household Furniture" as distinct from being a cabinetmaker — thus showing the change of emphasis to the selling side of the Furniture Industry.

It must be obvious that there was also considerable Continental influence which, over the years, moulded the English style of furniture. This showed itself blatantly in some ways, with the use of very French style motifs at one time, and of course even more widely in the Chinese, Greek and Italian influences which are apparent in the furniture of the 18th century. Often more subtle influences come into play which arose from the emigration of craftsmen, or from the export of furniture which, when seen in other countries, caused the client to seek a homemade version from a local craftsman. This was initially the case with America, which depended heavily on Europe for both craftsmen and imports. We tend to relate the export trade to the late 19th and the 20th centuries, but in 1680 the petition presented before Parliament, *The Case of the Cane Chair Makers,* it is recorded that "above two thousand dozens (of chairs) are yearly transported" showing how heavy was this early trade. In 1700, chairs to the value of £7,560 were exported from London to the American Colonies, an undertaking which had risen by 1888 to a total value of £746,000.

The colonies were a particularly fruitful source of income for the exporter, as although by the mid-18th century they had built up an expanding industry themselves, English furniture and furnishings were still in demand and were imported, or copied by American craftsmen. The *Massachusett's Gazeteer* of January 6th 1772 published the plea for "a genteel set of mahogany chamber chairs, with carv'd knees and claw feet (English made) or any other very neat good furniture" and in the *Boston Evening Post* of August 20th 1764, the reader is advised that Nathaniel Langdon has imported "A Compleat Assortment of Upholsterer's Goods... the best of the kind, and as he purchased them at the lowest rates in London, and will sell for small profits and only for present pay, the buyer may be sure for a good pennyworth".

Other Americans would buy direct from London or France according to taste. George Washington did not always remain loyal to American furniture, and in 1757 wrote to his London Agent, "Send me one dozen strong chairs of about 15 shillings apiece... I have one dozen chairs that were made in this country; neat but too weak for common setting". The emigrant was also a means of taking furniture styles to the far flung posts of the empire, for the idea of stocking up the cabin with furniture was essential. Sir M. Malcolm, writing in the 1820s, advises his daughters who are about to set out for India, "Your cabin furniture, if it has no other recommendation, is English, and will always have a value in proportion to your length of absence from England". Similarly when Charles Hursthouse was advising on emigration to New Zealand (1861) he adds, "As all articles in the cabin go freight free, passengers often crowd in things till they can scarcely get into bed or get out"!

By 1789 the Shakers had set up their chair factory at New Lebanon, and in 1795 the great American cabinetmaker, Duncan Phyfe, opened his shop in New York, but still the furniture imports from England continued:-

The Boston rocker c.1820-1850, which was made in England in the 1850s as the American Rocking Chair.

1783 £4,443
1784 £8,533

In 1817 an observer commented that "There are here several large carvers' and Gilders' shops, glass mirrors and picture frames are executed with taste and elegance; but still the most superior are imported from England". This could give a distorted picture however, as it was not entirely a one-way stream of traffic. It is perhaps true that most of the influence of America has been in the 19th and 20th centuries, but one of the most truly American chairs, the *rocker* was developed and came to England in the late Regency period, being made later in this country in 1850s and known as the *American Rocking Chair,* while in the low-back Windsor chair range, the introduction of the *smoker's bow* in the 1830s added a style which was made by the thousand for office and bar right into the 1930s.

Much of the furniture of the early 19th century fell under the heading of *American Empire* style, and with the early phase (1805-15) known as *American Directoire* it bore a strong resemblance to the work of the late Sheraton period and the English Regency. Several leading American cabinetmakers were of British origin, including Duncan Phyfe and John and Ephraim Haines, and often the English styles were adopted quite late, with *American Chippendale* in vogue until 1785 in the fashionable quarters, and in use in country districts up to fifty years after it had ceased to be popular in England. This reliance on English source-books changed dramatically a little later. Berry B. Tracy records that "After the War of 1812-14, the hatred of England turned the attention of many to French manners and taste", and the Continental influence was most noticeable, supported by the expertise of a number of craftsmen who arrived as French immigrants.

Among the native American features which made their furniture identifiable are the uses of certain methods and motifs, for instance the appearance of the double cornucopia infilling which represents the land of plenty, an expression echoing the words of Washington to Lafayette "We have opened the fertile plains of Ohio to the poor, unfortunate, the oppressed of the earth. All those who are overladen, broken down, seeking a soil to cultivate, may come and find the promised land flowing with milk and honey". Another feature is the replacement of the brass inlay, so beloved of the Regency craftsmen, by the use of stencil work, which has for so long been used extensively by the American cabinetmaker.

During the French Restoration period (1814-30) there were two main styles, the English-influenced designs which incorporated a wide range of rich carving and recoration, and the French orientated furniture which was created in a much plainer style. However, in the later Empire period of the late 1830s there was a deterioration in design, similar in many respects to that experienced in the

148

Victorian England of the 1870s, which seems to coincide with the early introduction of mass-produced furniture to meet the demands of the exploding market.

10 Upholstery

The furniture itself was not the only aspect of furnishing to be developed. The actual upholstery in use changed over the years. The embryo furniture of the 14th and 15th centuries was not normally upholstered, and as we know that silk, velvet, wool and linen were used in this country by that time, it is probable that some form of cushioning was in use. Embroidery was of a high quality at this time, but was chiefly employed for ecclesiastical vestments and furnishings. It is most probable that the early chests and benches in the halls were covered with cushions or with strips of cloth or velvet on which the lady of the house or her ladies in waiting might have embroidered the arms of the owner in gold thread. Although woollen cloth and linen was made in this country, this would be more in use with the lesser knights, with velvet being brought in to England from the Continent for use by the wealthy.

By the reign of Queen Elizabeth the method of making pile carpets was practised, a way copied from the east, hence the use of the term *Turkey Work*. The pile was made of wool and when small panels were woven they could be used for the coverings of seat and backs of chairs and settees. The designs in use at this time were often small floral sprays knotted in coloured wools, and in the reign of James I the weaving of silk fabrics, so as well as the *Turkey work* in use so far, the Farthingale chairs were covered in plain, figured or embroidered velvet and straight fringes were in use up to the mid 17th century. During the Protectorate Period, everything was as plain as possible, and chairs were usually upholstered in leather and studded with brass headed nails.

The velvets which were imported came chiefly from Italy. They were bold in design, and red was the favourite colour, sometimes on a ground of gold. The woodwork of the X-chair was often covered entirely with crimson or purple velvet, while the back panels were made of leather covered with velvet, decorated with an embroidered motif.

The padded seats, backs and arms were finished off with a short fringe of silk and gold thread, and the design of wavy stems of leaves and fruit was common. The early tapestry looms were believed to have been set up in the middle of the 16th century, and William Sheldon, who set up at Barcheston and in Warwickshire was among the earliest. Immigrant Flemish weavers were probably chiefly involved, but the designs were typically English with small flowers and fresh colours. The cushions which were used with the plainer wainscot chairs and the Derbyshire chairs were often covered on the underside

150

William and Mary period upholstered settee.

with leather, and a short tufted fringe ran around the edge with knotted tassels at the corners.

During the reign of James I the upholstered settee appeared in this country and for the first time the whole was covered with velvet or damask, finished off with a straight fringe. The large surface was usually converted into panels by the use of flat *galloons* of gold thread, a kind of narrow close woven ribbon used for trimming. With the Restoration the demand of the Court for rich fabrics could still not be met by the looms of England, so for some twenty years, velvets, silks, damasks, and brocatelles were imported from Florence, Genoa and Lyons. The designs were still chiefly plant and floral motifs, but the embroidery for the coverings of settees, chairs and stools was of *Hungarian point* and patterns of zig-zag lines in yellow and shades of green worked in floss silks covered the whole of the ground. The use of close-fitting covers which could be provided with hooks and eyes for removal was just beginning, and in the early Queen Anne period the *slip-seat,* which could be slipped out of the seat frame, was in use, often covered with petit point or tapestry.

Towards the end of the 17th century more elaborate upholstery appeared, largely influenced by Continental styles. From the looms of Lyons came damasks, brocades and velvets in designs which were symmetrical in form, together with velvets made of three or four colours, or the *terry-velvet* which had the surface partly left in uncut loops, while others had a pattern stamped on the pile. Following the revocation of the *Edict of Nantes* in 1685 many French weavers sought refuge in England, and in time Spitalfields became the chief weaving centre for damasks and brocades, rivalling that of Lyons. The designs were French in style and it was only with the accession of William III that furniture and upholstery became simpler and the Dutch influence was felt.

Queen Anne settee with cabriole legs.

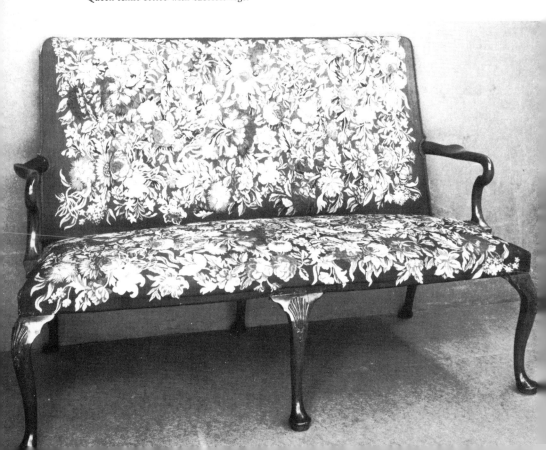

Late 18th century sofa of Grecian couch shape.

During the early years of the 18th century needlework was used widely for chair-coverings. Designs in *petit-point* and *gross-point* gave emphasis to the design and the panels were made in shapes to fit the backs, seats and the sides of the chairs. The motifs were still largely floral, although the use of rural scenes with shepherdesses were coming into vogue. The heavy chairs of the William Kent period, with their rich gilding, brought into use silk damasks and velvets, woven at Spitalfields but still quite Continental in character. The increased use of upholstered settees which were embroidered in mythological subjects were now worked in perspective and the pictures of famous artists were copied on the tapestries and furniture. The designs were worked in *gros-point*, *petit-point* and *cross stitch* on canvas in coloured silks and wools.

The mid 18th century saw the interest in striped and wavy line patterns. Robert Adam introduced classical designs from Italy and the fabrics came from the mills in the same designs for use on furniture upholstery. By 1760 *chintz* printing for materials for use by the upholsterer was being produced by block printing and engraved copper plates. During the end of the 18th century the influence of the Empire Style and the effect of Napoleon's campaign in Egypt

153

(1789-99) had as much influence on fabrics as on furniture design. The patterns created for the silk damasks and brocades used the classical ornaments of the palm, the olive, honeysuckle, and acanthus, with vases and medallions in symmetrical arrangement. Also in this period the gilt chairs and settees beloved by Adam and those who espoused the French style were covered still with tapestry, and it is probable, that as the weaving of tapestry in England was not great at this time, most would have come from France with panels of animals and figures in oval medallions festooned with flowers, woven on a cream or green background.

The use of upholstery had always been an added enrichment to furniture, and from the earliest days, the panels of embroidered or woven materials were treasured, and even transferred from chair to chair as the occasion arose. The late 18th century saw a change in this attitude. Firstly, the copper engraved plate was introduced in 1770 which, being incised, allowed a greater closeness of detail and the production of line prints which were almost equal to the engravings from which they were copied. Then in 1793 the engraved roller was introduced and a machine could produce 4,000 yards a day, equalling the output of over forty block printers in the same time. By 1801 the arduous task of hand engraving the plates and rollers was revolutionised by mechanical engraving, so with the roller printing machine, the day of expensive fabrics had gone, and the richer finishes were brought within the reach of a much wider range of customer.

The Age of Mechanisation was just around the corner, and William Morris' twin concept "have nothing in your home that you do not know to be useful or believe to be beautiful" was at last becoming a possibility for the masses.

Bibliography

Bernasconi, J.R. *The English Domestic Chair*. 1977.

Binstead, H.E. *English Chairs*. 1923.

Boger, L.A. *The Complete Guide to Furniture Styles*. 1961.

Boynton, L.O.J. *The Bed Bug and the Age of Elegance*. Furniture History (1965).

Cescinsky, H. & Gribble, E.R. *Early English Furniture and Woodwork*. Vol.1. 1922.

Darty, P. *Chairs*. 1972.

Eames, P. *Furniture in England, France and the Netherlands from the 12th to 15th Centuries*. 1977.

Edwards, R. *The Dictionary of English Furniture*. 1954.

Geller, J.A. *The History of Children's Furniture*. Mss. 1978 (High Wycombe Library).

Gloag, J.E. *The Englishman's Chair*. 1964.

Harvey, J. *Mediaeval Craftsmen*. 1975.

Harrison, J. *The History of English Furniture*. 1972.

Hayward, J.F. *Tables in the Victoria and Albert Museum*. 1961.

Hayward, J.F. *English Cabinets in the Victoria and Albert Museum*. 1964.

Hopkinson, J. *Memories of a Victorian Cabinet Maker*. 1968.

Joy, E.T. *The County Life Book of Chairs*. 1967.

Mackay, J. *Nursery Antiques*. 1976.

Roe, F. *Ancient Coffers and Cupboards*. 1902.

Roe, G.F. *Windsor Chairs*. 1953.

Salzman, L.F. *Building in England Down to 1540*. 1952.

Sparkes, I.G. *The English Country Chair*. 1973.

Sparkes, I.G. *The Windsor Chair*. 1975.

Symonds, R.W. *The Bed from Saxon to Victorian Times*. Country Life Annual (1951).

Synge, L. *Chairs in Colour*. 1978.

Toller, J. *Antique Miniature Furniture in Great Britain and America*. 1966.

Wolsey, S.W. & Luff, R.W.P. *Furniture in England: The Age of the Joiner*. 1968.

Wright, L. Warm and Snug: *The History of the Bed*. 1962.

A more detailed bibliography, including periodical articles, can be obtained from The Wycombe Chair Museum, Priory Avenue, High Wycombe, Bucks.

Glossary of the Lesser Known Terms

Acanthus Leaf carving: carving which copied the foliage on the Corinthian Greek pillar capitals.

Ball feet: a turned foot in the form of a ball used on chest of drawers etc.

Baluster turning: a leg or spindle turning which used rings, beads and the vase shaped sections.

Barrel frieze: the outward swelling round horizontal frieze found below the cornice of a cabinet or high bookcase.

Bombé shape: a French term for the pronounced outward swell towards the base found in the side elevations of 18th century commodes and other cabinet furniture.

Bosses: projecting carved ornaments — often round in shape.

Bracket foot: a low plinth-like foot used on desks and chests of drawers.

Bun feet: small round feet flattened at the bottom and the top used on desks and cabinets.

Cabriole leg: a curved leg with a strongly projecting knee, often lavishly carved and terminated with a pad, claw & ball or other decorated foot.

Card-cut lattice work: fret-work patterns cut in low relied on a solid background.

Chevron pattern: an inverted V-pattern used in a zig-zag way as a border, often carved or used in inlay work.

Chip-carving: simple decoration used on chests and cupboard doors from the medieval period with geometrical or flower patterns marked with compasses and rulers and then chipped out with a knife or chisel.

Claw and ball feet: a leg terminal ending in an animals claw set on a round ball, used chiefly on cabriole legs.

Club feet: a leg terminal ending with the carved foot resting on a flat circular disc.

Cup and cover turning: a heavy melon shaped turning used on bedposts and table legs in Tudor and Stuart period with the lower swelling like the shape of a cup on a stem, and the cover or lid carved just above it.

Escalloped: an indented edge, patterned like the scallop shell.

Fielded panels: a door or cabinet panel with a flat centre set proud of its bevelled edge and often raised above the level of the surrounding framework.

Gadrooning: decoration in the form of a series of concave or convex petal-like carvings, often found on lid edges or on the cup section of cup and cover leg turnings.

Hinges: Butt hinge set into the door so that only the thin column of the actual hinge can be seen; a rule hinge is used on a dropping flap and use of concave and convex edges on the timber sections and prevents it being seen when the flap is dropped; The cocks-head hinge has elaborate outlines likened to a cockerel's head; a strap hinge has a very long decorative plate for fixing it to doors or cabinets or chests and this is fully visible; butterfly hinge dates back to medieval times and has wings like a butterfly.

Lap dovetail: is used on drawer fronts and the lap or flap hides the dovetail which is set back from the surface of the drawer.

Linenfold pattern: a vertical carving of folds of linen in use since the 15th century.

Ogee shape: a carving used as a moulding which is in a long S-shape.

Ovolo bars: a quarter-round moulded with lips used in glazing.

Parchemin pattern: used on panels since 16th century with a broad X-shape filling the centre of the panel infilled with ivy leaves and grapes.

Pediments: the top rail of a tall bookcase or cabinet — Broken pediment has a break in the centre in which a small pedestal is fitted to take an urn or bust; a swan necked pediment is similar except that the sides of the opening are formed into S-shape curves named swan-neck curves.

Sabre leg: a square sectioned leg which resembles the wide sweeped curve of a sabre.

Serpentine shape: a wave-like shape used for shaping the front of commodes or desks.

Tusk-tenoned: a woodworking joint where a tenon is pushed through the mortise hole and protrudes beyond the other end and is then wedged into position.

Voluted caps: a spiral scroll ornament similar to the capital of the Ionic style, also called ears — used on the scrolled ends of a Windsor chair comb.

Index

WITHDRAWN